SESE History Book 6
Helena Gannon

The Educational Company of Ireland

Note for Teachers and Parents

History Window On the World is a series of history books for third to sixth class. Using this series, children are encouraged to be active agents exploring the past. **History Window On the World** encourages them to be curious and excited about history while investigating and analysing primary sources. They work as historians, analysing primary sources such as documentary, pictorial, artefactual and oral evidence.

History Window On the World is in line with the Revised Curriculum and contains the appropriate strands and strand units for each class level. Children acquire the necessary knowledge and concepts while developing relevant skills and attitudes. **History Window On the World** allows for the investigation of personal, family and local history while learning about other significant historical topics.

History Window On the World allows children to learn in a fun and exciting way. They will also develop an understanding of attitudes, beliefs and motivations of people in the past and gain a better insight into our world today. The development of historical skills encourages children to view situations from other people's perspectives.

Assessment is a key component of the **History Window On the World** series. There are four elements of assessment:
- **Question Time** uses lower and higher order questions to assess children's understanding of information while helping to develop higher order thinking skills.
- **Creative Time** stimulates children's imagination while also allowing children to develop empathy with characters from the past. It also encourages them to explore history on another level through poetry, drama, music or art.
- **Puzzle Time** provides fun activities for reinforcing information.
- **Time Detective** enables children to develop relevant skills while actively exploring the past.

The use of IT skills is catered for in the series with website references for teachers, parents and children to investigate. **Web Watch!** indicates a link to further information and page 111 contains **Web References** for each chapter in the book. Guided by the teacher or parent, children can explore each topic in greater detail and develop the skills of an historian in a fun and informative way.

Each chapter ends with a page dedicated to integration which is central to the Revised Curriculum. The teacher and pupils are provided with a wide array of ideas for integrating the topic into other subject areas, reinforcing the knowledge learned. A comprehensive Teacher's Resource Book is available with extra activities, ICT suggestions and photocopiable material.

We hope that children will enjoy using **History Window On the World** and that the skills of being an historian will give them pleasure and a life-long treasure.

Helena Gannon

Contents

Chapter	Topic	Strand	Strand Unit	Page
1	My Locality through the Ages	Local studies	My locality through the ages	4
2	Farming through the Ages	Continuity and change over time	Farming	10
3	Native Americans	Early people and ancient societies	North American peoples	18
4	The Healing Waters	Story	Myths and legends	26
5	The Maoris	Early people and ancient societies	Australasian peoples	33
6	The Renaissance	Eras of change and conflict	The Renaissance	40
7	Remembering School	Local studies	Schools	46
8	The Liberator	Politics, conflict and society	O'Connell and Catholic Emancipation	54
9	Planes, Trains and Automobiles	Continuity and change over time	Transport	62
10	World War I	Eras of change and conflict	World War I	70
11	The Emergency	Life, society, work and culture in the past	Life during World War II	80
12	Children of War	Story	Stories from the lives of people in the past	90
13	Ireland, the EU and the UN	Politics, conflict and society	Ireland, Europe and the world, 1960 to the present	96
14	Heroes from the Past	Working as an historian		104
15	Quiz Time	Revision		108
16	Web References	Research	Project work	111
17	Timeline	Working as an historian		112

1 My Locality through the Ages

Every locality has its own history. Working as an historian, investigate the history of your local area.

- What was it like to live there in the past?
- What changes have occurred over the years?
- What has stayed the same?

Older people in your locality can help you to gather this information. Photographs give us a good insight into the past. Study these two photographs carefully and answer the following questions.

Lismore, Co. Waterford, 1880

Lismore, Co. Waterford, today

1. How has Lismore changed over the years?
2. What buildings are the same?
3. How have the road surface and road markings changed?
4. What methods of transport were used in the past?

Children investigate primary sources to explore the history of their local area.

Get Interviewing!

Invite older members of your locality, or a local historian, to visit your class. Prepare some questions before their visit. Remember to include questions that encourage them to share their memories. Record their answers.

Some questions to help you to get started:

- How has the locality changed over the years?
- What has stayed the same?
- What new developments have happened in recent years?

- Have the roads and road markings changed over the years?
- Have the methods of transport changed over the years?
- Have any important events occurred while you lived in this locality?

- What is your favourite memory of the local area?
- What shops were there in the area?
- What was your favourite place in the locality?

- Where did people work?
- Do you have any stories, legends or songs about the local area?
- Were there any local clubs?

Primary Sources

Historians investigate primary sources to get a picture of life in the past. Working as an historian, gather some primary sources about your locality. Local libraries are an excellent resource.

Investigate!

- **Maps** of your locality allow you to discover what your area looked like in the past.
- **Local newspapers** may have some interesting articles about important events from the past.
- **Photographs** provide us with a window into the past.
- **Placenames** give us important information about our locality.
- **Monuments and plaques** give us details about important historic events.

> **Word Watch!**
> **Primary sources**
> Items such as photographs, diaries, letters or newspapers are called primary sources. They are recorded or written at the time of the event.
>
> **Secondary sources** are items such as books or articles written at a later date, after the events have taken place.

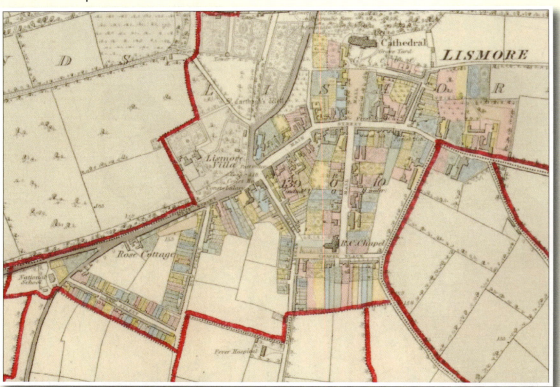

A map of Lismore, Co. Waterford, 1829–41

Using a digital camera take some photographs for your project.

Project Time!

Present your findings in a class display. Include old and more recent photographs of your locality.

Some questions to investigate:

1. Who were the first people to settle in your area?
2. Why, do you think, did they settle there?
3. Why was your village or town given its name?
4. Were any important battles fought in your locality?
5. Did any important events occur in your area?
6. Were any famous people born in your locality?
7. Are there any old buildings, such as houses, mills, or factories in your area?
8. Was there a workhouse in your area?
9. Are there any old stories, legends, or songs written about your area?

Question Time

1. What is a primary source? Give **one** example of a primary source.
2. What are secondary sources? Give **one** example of a secondary source.
3. Give **three** examples of information about your locality that you could gather from older people in your area.
4. What information can you get from investigating old newspapers?
5. Give **two** reasons why photographs are important to an historian.
6. What is the purpose of monuments and plaques?
7. Think of some famous people living today. Would you like to see a monument erected for one of them? Give reasons for your answer.

Creative Time

1. Draw a plan of your locality in the future. What changes and developments do you think will take place? Will there be any new roads, buildings or other development? How, do you think, could your locality be improved? Draw up blueprints for your locality of the future. Include pictures.
2. Create a class book of local stories, ballads and songs. Interview older members of the community and record their memories.

Puzzle Time

Write 'primary source' or 'secondary source' after each of the following:

diary _____	newspapers _____
history book _____	letter _____
photograph _____	biography _____

Time Detective

Working as an historian, create a timeline for your locality. Include any important historic events, battles or developments that occurred.

Web Watch!

To see projects about different localities in Ireland, visit:
http://www.rootsweb.ancestry.com/~nirfer/
http://www.irelandgenweb.com/special.htm

Integration Project

My Locality through the Ages

English
Write a letter to your local councillor or TD, drawing their attention to the needs of your locality. What areas need attention or improvement? Include your own suggestions.

Gaeilge
An Baile Mór: I ngrúpaí beaga: beidh siopa nó bialann ag gach grúpa. Siúlann tú timpeall an bhaile ag ceannach rudaí sna siopaí nó ag díol. Dúnann gach siopa ag am difriúil don lón.

Mathematics
Using your local bus timetable, answer the following questions:
- How many hours and minutes are there from the departure time of the first bus to the departure time of the last bus?
- How many buses are there per hour?
- How long does it take the bus to get to its destination?
- What time is the first bus you could get after school?

Drama
Create a short advertisement for your locality, encouraging tourists to visit. What local attractions will you include? Working in small groups, make your local area as attractive as possible.

Geography
Design a new park for your locality. What amenities will be included? Draw up a plan for your park, considering the needs of your local area. Powerpoint could be used to present your design.

SPHE
Organise an election for a mayor of your class. Write a speech to convince your classmates to vote for you. Why would you be the best candidate for the job? What changes would you make? How would you make your classroom a better place? How would you make your local area a better place?

Art
Working in small groups, create a model of your locality. Each group could make a different building or landmark. Use cardboard boxes, paper, glue and paint to recreate a model of your area.

Science
Carry out an environmental assessment of your locality. Investigate pollution, noise, traffic, litter, graffiti and green spaces. Give recommendations for ways in which your locality could be improved.

2 Farming Through the Ages

8000 BC–6000 BC

8000 BC–6000 BC
People gradually changed from hunting to farming as a way of living. Jericho, in the Middle East, had one of the first farming communities. Barley, wheat, peas and lentils were grown there. The people tamed some of the wild animals and used them for working on their farms.

4000 BC
The first farmers arrived in Ireland. People grew crops and kept animals such as goats, sheep and cattle.

4000 BC

3500 BC
Oxen were used to plough the fields. The first fields were square-shaped because farmers had to plough the fields twice. This cross-ploughing made the fields ready for sowing.

3500 BC

1000 BC
The Celts arrived in Ireland. They brought new iron tools with them. They also had new customs and traditions.

1000 BC

Children examine continuity and change in farming through the ages in a line of development study.

1973
Ireland joined the EEC. It became easier for Irish farmers to sell their food to other European countries.

1973

1890s
The first tractors were built. When farmers could afford them, they replaced their horses with tractors.

1890s

1700s
In Europe, horses replaced oxen on farms. They were used to pull new heavy equipment such as the plough and the harrow.

1700s

1600s

1600s
The arrival of the potato from America changed the Irish diet. Potatoes were easy to grow and nutritious and Irish people soon became dependent on them.

1169 AD

1169 AD
The Normans introduced new farming methods to Ireland such as haymaking. They brought their cattle in for shelter during the winter and fed them hay.

Farming Artefacts

Study each of the farming artefacts very carefully.

1. What was the artefact made from?
2. How might it have been used?
3. What is used today to do the same work?
4. Draw the modern version of each farming tool.

Technology and Change

For many years, basic farming methods did not change very much. The earliest tools used by farmers were made of bones, stone and wood. In the past, Irish farmers grew wheat, barley and oats. An ox was used to pull a wooden plough. Later, a horse was used. In the past, farming communities helped each other with their farming tasks. Today, machinery is used to do most of the work. This has meant that fewer people are now employed on farms. The agricultural revolution of the 1700s brought huge changes to farming in Europe. There was a demand for more food. Fields had previously been left fallow (empty) to keep the soil fertile. Now, the planting of crops was rotated. This meant that more crops could be grown in a year.

Tractors over the Years

1916 – Fordson Tractor

Allis Chalmers Tractor

Compare these tractors from the past with modern tractors. What developments have taken place over the years? Compare the wheels of the tractors in terms of style and function. What is the most significant development that has happened over the years?

Science and Farming

Today, science plays a useful role in farming developments. Fertilisers and sprays are used more often by farmers. Organic farmers prefer to use natural methods only for growing crops. Scientific breeding and genetic engineering allow livestock and crops to grow larger and faster. Genetic engineering has allowed scientists to develop fruit that ripens more slowly or has a built-in resistance to insects.

Genetic Engineering

Scientists can change the way that plants and animals reproduce. This is called genetic engineering. Some people are opposed to it. They feel that it allows scientists to create or change plants and animals in a way that is not natural. They believe that there is not enough scientific understanding of the effect that genetic engineering may have on the environment and on our health.

Dairy Farming

Technology has played an enormous role in helping the dairy farmer. In the past, cows were milked by hand. This was a slow process. Today, cows are milked in milking parlours and machines do the work. Computers keep records of each cow's milk supply. These machines have revolutionised dairy farming. Refrigeration has also helped by keeping the milk fresh. However, in developing countries, most milking is still done by hand.

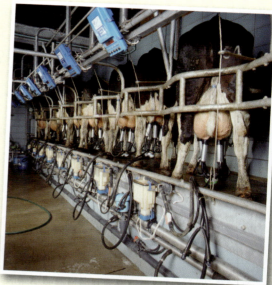

Farming Statistics

	1911	2005
Number of farmers	780,867	132,700
Male farmers	721,669	120,000
Female farmers	59,198	12,700

Study the statistics from 1911 and 2005. Answer the following questions:
1. Why, do you think, has there been a decrease in the number of farmers in Ireland?
2. What did you find interesting about the statistics?
3. Were you surprised by the statistics?

Question Time

1. Where was the first farming community located?
2. What crops did the first farmers grow?
3. When did the first farmers arrive in Ireland?
4. What changes did the Normans introduce to farming in Ireland?
5. Why did the arrival of the potato have such a huge influence on the Irish diet?
6. When were the first tractors built?
7. List ways in which developments in technology have helped farmers in their daily work.
8. How many farmers were there in Ireland in 1911?

Creative Time

1. Design a farming machine of the future.

   - What will this machine do?
   - How will it help the daily life of a farmer?

   Label your design, giving details about how it operates.

2. Design a poster encouraging safety on the farm. What are the most important points to consider?

Puzzle Time

1. Unscramble the following farming tools:

thecsy	_____	ghoulp	_____
lickes	_____	exa	_____
wohrar	_____	atocrtr	_____

2 Wordsearch

Find the following words in the wordsearch.

- agriculture
- barley
- fallow
- harrow
- Jericho
- oats
- oxen
- plough
- scythe
- sickle
- tractor
- wheat

Y	I	F	J	G	Z	Y	N	W	L	X	N	G	V	O
N	O	D	A	I	D	H	Z	B	A	R	L	E	Y	C
X	C	P	X	B	W	H	E	A	T	E	U	Q	S	N
S	J	E	R	I	C	H	O	K	R	E	D	A	D	T
W	O	R	R	A	H	A	C	U	A	S	Y	Y	U	P
L	F	Z	Z	O	O	U	T	I	C	I	X	J	F	O
L	Y	R	F	A	O	L	J	Y	T	J	D	C	N	X
Z	W	U	T	A	U	D	T	P	O	E	N	J	T	P
W	Z	S	M	C	L	H	W	I	R	J	C	F	L	L
W	U	G	I	L	E	L	R	H	G	U	O	L	P	W
W	X	R	H	J	F	I	O	F	J	S	N	T	C	H
N	G	O	W	A	W	D	P	W	O	W	B	M	R	P
A	X	S	J	P	R	X	E	M	X	Z	H	O	D	V
Y	V	S	I	C	K	L	E	S	E	F	A	B	N	O
T	V	I	V	Q	P	H	Y	D	N	F	O	K	H	Y

Time Detective

Invite local farmers into your class to talk about their memories of farming in the past. Write some questions you would like to ask them about the changes in farming over the years. Investigate farmhouses in your area. How have they changed over time? Are there any organic farmers in your area? Present your findings in a report, or create a poster called 'Farming in my Locality'.

Web Watch!

http://www.historyforkids.org/learn/economy/farming/
http://www.dmoz.org/Kids_and_Teens/School_Time/Science/Farming/
http://www.teagasc.ie
http://www.esatclear.ie/~turoefarm/top/farms.htm

Integration Project

English
Create a big book of farming for sharing with younger classes in your school. Working together, write the book as a class. Then work in pairs, with each pair making a different page of the book

Gaeilge
Fiche ceist: Smaoiníonn páiste ar rud éigin atá ar an bhfeirm. Cuir ceisteanna air/uirthi chun an rud a thomhas. Tá cead fiche ceist a chur.

Mathematics
The perimeter of a field is 456m. If the length of the field is 152m, what is the area of the field?

Drama
A local farmer has offered his field to be used for genetic engineering. A meeting has been called in the Community Hall to discuss this. In groups, take on the role of different parties in the debate such as environmentalists, scientists, farmers and local residents.

Farming through the Ages

Geography
It is important that we use sustainable energy. Wind farms are a renewable energy source. Choose a suitable site in your area for a wind farm. Give reasons for your choice. Consider the impact of a wind farm on the local environment.

Music
Divide your class into groups. Each group is given a word related to farming. The group must sing a song that contains that word. If the group sings a song containing the word, the team earns five points. The team with the most points wins.

Art
Create a farm collage. Use items such as fabric, wool, string, felt and cotton wool to make the collage.

Science
Learn more about plants while helping Detective Leplant solve the mystery of the Great Plant Escape at

http://www.urbanext.uiuc.edu/gpe/index.html

3 Native Americans

The first people to live in North America were Native Americans. Over 15,000 years ago, they travelled on foot from Asia to North America. The two continents were linked by a land bridge made of ice. The sea eventually rose and covered the land bridge. This sea is known today as the Bering Strait.

The Native Americans spread right across America and formed into different groups called tribes.

Arctic Tribes such as the Inuit.

Northwest Coast Tribes such as Chinook and Haida.

California Tribes such as the Maidu and Hupa.

Southwest Tribes such as the Apache and Navajo.

Eastern Woodland Tribes such as the Iroquois, Chippewa, Chickasaw and Cherokee.

Plains Tribes such as the Sioux, Comanche, Cheyenne, Crow and Blackfoot.

The Native American tribes adapted to the places they settled. Each tribe had a different language, culture and lifestyle. Their lifestyle depended on where they lived, the natural resources available to them and the climate that they experienced.

Children explore aspects of the lives of the Native American people.

Homes

Native Americans lived in many different types of homes depending on the climate and lifestyle of their tribe. Tribes that moved from place to place, in order to hunt, needed homes that could be built easily and were easy to move. Tribes living in colder climates needed homes to protect them from the weather. Their homes were made from natural resources found around them such as wood, animal skins and grass.

Teepee

The teepee was home to the Native Americans of the Plains. It was made of long, wooden poles covered in animal skins. The poles could be easily taken down and moved quickly to follow the buffalo herd. Sometimes the teepees were arranged in a circle. A flap was used as a doorway.

Longhouse

Longhouses were made of wooden poles covered with tree bark. They were rectangular in shape. They were home to the Eastern Woodland tribes. Several families lived together in one longhouse.

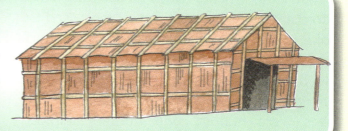

Wigwam

Some Woodland tribes built wigwams. They were round in shape and were made from logs covered with bark.

Chickee

Chickees were built with logs. The roofs were made with palm trees or grass. There were no walls and they were built on a platform to prevent flooding.

Clothing

Different tribes wore different clothes. Clothes were made by hand and decorated with artwork such as beads and pictures. Tribes made clothes from deer skins and buffalo hides. They wore leather shoes called moccasins. Native American men wore breechcloths. These were long pieces of cloth or hide tucked over a belt. In some tribes, men wore kilts or fur trousers. Native American women wore skirts and leggings or dresses. The design and length differed from tribe to tribe. Each tribe wore different types of headwear.

Food

Native Americans used food that was available to them. Corn was the main ingredient of most meals. It could be used to make many different foods. Beans and squash were also eaten. Wild plants, fruit and nuts were gathered. Fishing was also very important to Native Americans. Some tribes were hunters and hunted animals such as buffalo, deer, goats, rabbits or bears.

New Settlers

Imagine that you belong to a Native American tribe. You have just settled in a region in North America. Describe the region that you have settled in.
- Investigate your area, researching the climate and the resources available.
- Design a house suitable for your climate and using local materials.
- What food might you eat?
- What clothes might you wear?
- What type of lifestyle will you have?

Hunters and Farmers

The tribes of the Eastern Woodlands were farmers. When they settled in a new area, the woodlands had to be cleared for farming. Crops such as corn, squash and beans were grown. The Iroquois tribe grew over fifteen types of corn and sixty types of beans.

The tribes of the Plains were hunters who depended on the buffalo. They moved from place to place following the buffalo. Almost every part of the buffalo was used in some way – for food, clothes, ropes, making teepees and tools. Basket making was an important part of the daily life of Native Americans.

For the tribes of the Arctic region, it was too cold for farming. They depended on hunting and fishing for food.

The tribes of the North West fished for salmon.

Games

Native Americans relaxed by playing games. Lacrosse was a very popular game. Each player had a wooden stick with a net at the end, which they used to catch and throw the ball. They tried to carry the ball to the goal at the end of the field. Sometimes, games went on for a full day – they could become quite violent! Shooting arrows and foot racing were also popular games.

Europeans Arrive

When European settlers arrived in North America, they called the Native Americans Indians. The Europeans believed that they had reached Asia and were now in India. The arrival of the Europeans brought many changes. The Native Americans were slowly pushed off their lands into special areas called reservations. The Europeans carried diseases such as smallpox and measles. Many Native Americans became sick and died. The Europeans took away the homes and hunting ground of the Native Americans. They slaughtered millions of buffalo, which left some tribes without any food.

Sitting Bull

Many tribes tried to fight back against the Europeans. Sitting Bull was a member of the Sioux tribe living on the Plains. He was chosen as chief in the wars against the white settlers on the Plains in the 1860s and 1870s. He led his people into war against General Custer in the Battle of the Little Bighorn. The Sioux won the battle but the American army was determined to get revenge. The tribes of the Plains were hunted down and forced into reservations.

Today, it is believed that there are over two million Native Americans living in America and a further one million living in Canada. They try to keep the customs and traditions of their culture alive.

Question Time

1. Who were the first people to live in America?
2. How did they reach the continent of America?
3. Name **two** Eastern Woodland tribes.
4. Name **two** tribes of the Great Plains.
5. How did the environment influence the way of life of the different tribes?
6. What is a teepee?
7. What is the difference between a wigwam and a teepee?
8. What clothes did female Native Americans wear?
9. What food did Native Americans eat?
10. Why were Native Americans called Indians by the Europeans?
11. Do you think that Native Americans were treated fairly by the European settlers?
12. What is the population of Native Americans living in North America today?

Creative Time

1. Totem poles were made by the Native Americans to show their family spirit and history. Working in small groups, create a class totem pole. Each group has a cardboard box. Decorate the cardboard box to resemble an animal head. Examples of animals used on totem poles are beavers, otters, bears, eagles, moose, seals, wolves and goats. Draw a different animal head on each box. Ears, wings and arms can be added to the side or back of the box. Feathers, beaks and paint can also be added. Using masking tape, the cardboard boxes can be stuck together, with the largest at the bottom and the smallest at the top.

Materials needed: cardboard boxes of different sizes, glue, masking tape, paper, paint, feathers and scissors.

2 Native Americans were given names that reflected aspects of their personality such as their talents and skills. Some Native American names are Running Deer, Black Hawk and Morning Star. Think up a Native American name for yourself that reflects something about you.

Puzzle Time

Crossword

Across

2 The land bridge the first Native Americans walked across from Asia (6, 6)
6 The main food used by Native Americans in most meals (4)
7 A house made of logs built on a platform (7)
9 The tribes of the Plains hunted for this animal (7)
10 An Arctic tribe (5)

Down

1 Chief of the Sioux tribe who fought against the white settlers (7, 4)
3 Home to the Native Americans of the Plains as it could be easily moved from place to place (6)
4 Popular game played with wooden sticks (8)
5 Leather shoes worn by Native Americans (9)
8 An Eastern Woodland tribe (7)

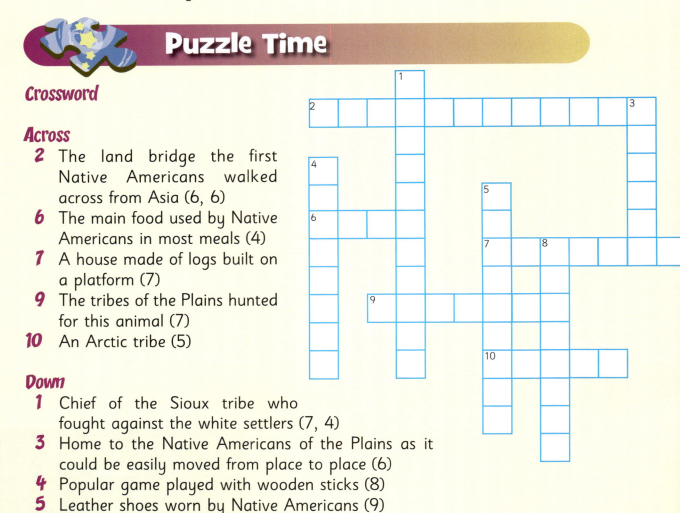

Time Detective

In 1847, the Native American Choctaw tribe made a donation to those suffering in the Great Famine in Ireland. They donated $710 to help starving men, women and children in Ireland. This donation would be worth $100,000 at today's values.

Find out more information about the Choctaw tribe and their donation to Ireland.

Web Watch!

To play some Native American games, visit:
http://www.mce.k12tn.net/indians/games/native_american_games.htm

Integration Project

Native Americans

English Oral Work
Read Native American myths and legends. Tell your favourite story or myth to the class. For a selection of stories, visit:
http://nativeamericans.mrdonn.org/stories/index.html

Gaeilge
Déan agallamh le Sitting Bull faoin gcogadh leis na daoine nua. Ag obair i mbeirteanna, cuir ceist air faoina shaol agus faoinar tharla dá mhuintir.

Mathematics
Round the population figures for Native American tribes to the nearest 1,000. For more information, visit:
http://www.americanwest.com/pages/indrank.htm

English
A diamante poem is written in the shape of a diamond. The first line has one word and increases until the fourth line, and then it gets smaller again. Write a diamante poem about Native Americans. For help, visit:
http://www.readwritethink.org/materials/diamante/

Geography
Choose a location in America where a Native American tribe lived. Give four clues to help your classmates to find your location.

Physical Education
Organise a lacrosse league for your class. Make a lacrosse stick by attaching a net to the end of a stick. Using your stick, pass the ball to your team mate and try to score goals.

Art
Create a model Native American village. Working in pairs, each pair builds a model of one of the different kinds of Native American homes. Use natural materials such as twigs, grass, and bark for your building.

Science
Native Americans treat their plant life with respect and care. Investigate the plant life in your locality. Make a booklet with information about different plants and flowers. Draw pictures or gather photographs to put into your booklet.

4 The Healing Waters

In your opinion, what does this Native American proverb mean?

> 'Treat the earth well. It was not given to you by your parents; it was loaned to you by your children. We do not inherit the earth from our ancestors; we borrow it from our children.'

Native Americans loved to tell stories. Stories were passed down from one generation to the next. Many stories were told to teach people about how important nature and the earth are. The story of *The Healing Waters* is a legend from the Iroquois tribe.

Once there lived a great Iroquois warrior named Nekumonta. He had always had great respect for the animals, plants and flowers of the forest.

It was winter time and the snow lay deep on the ground. The Native Americans were suffering from sickness and disease. A deadly plague had come to the village, killing many people. Nekumonta had lost almost all his family to the plague. His wife Shanewis, lay dying from the illness.

> I must find the healing herbs that the great God Manitou has planted. I will bring them back to you.

Shanewis saw the spirits of her friends who had died from the plague. They called to her and asked her to join them. Her husband begged her not to give up. He set out on a difficult mission to find healing herbs that could cure her illness.

Children explore a Native American myth and express the story through music, drama and art.

For three days and nights, Nekumonta searched the forest. He waded through rivers and climbed over hills. He searched deep in the snow for the healing herbs.

"Where will I find the healing herbs Manitou has planted?"

Nekumonta met a rabbit. He asked the rabbit to help him to find the healing herbs. But the rabbit did not reply and ran away.

Later, Nekumonta met a bear. He begged the bear to tell him where to find the cure. But the bear wandered off without answering.

On the third night, Nekumonta was weak and ill. He stumbled over a branch and fell down on the snow. He was too tired to get up. He closed his eyes and went to sleep.

While he slept, the animals of the forest gathered. They remembered his kindness to them. They called on the Great Manitou to help Nekumonta. Manitou heard the calls of the animals. He took pity on Nekumonta.

"He has always respected plants and trees and he has shown great kindness to us."

"We must call on the Great Manitou to help him."

That night the Great Spirit came to Nekumonta in his dream. He saw a beautiful waterfall and heard a sweet song.

Find the healing waters of Manitou and your wife shall be saved.

The healing waters might be underground, beneath the snow.

When Nekumonta woke up, he set off to look for the waterfall. He searched high and low but he could not find any water.

Nekumonta dug for hours. The animals watched. Nekumonta was exhausted. Just as he was about to give up, he saw a trickle of water. He began to dig with new-found energy and finally he found the hidden spring.

I must take this water back to Shanewis before it is too late!

Nekumonta drank from the spring and his strength returned. He was no longer tired.

Nekumonta filled a clay pot with the healing water.

He rushed back home to his wife. He ran as fast as he could. He hoped that he was not too late.

> We are saved! We are saved!

The villagers raced out of their homes to greet him.

Nekumonta ran to his wife. She was close to death. He poured the water into her mouth and watched as she fell asleep. When she woke up, she was completely cured.

> We must always respect the animals and plants for they have saved our village.

Nekumonta told the villagers where to find the healing waters. Soon, the whole village was free of the plague. The people of the village thanked Nekumonta. He told them that it was the animals who had helped him. Since then, the Native Americans have always respected plants and animals.

Question Time

1. What tribe did Nekumonta belong to?
2. What tragedy came to the village?
3. What mission did Nekumonta set out on?
4. How, do you think, did Nekumonta feel before setting out on his journey?
5. Why was it so difficult to find the healing herbs?
6. Who was Manitou?
7. Why did the animals help Nekumonta in his search?
8. How did Nekumonta learn about the healing waters?
9. Where did he find the healing waters?
10. How did Nekumonta carry the water home to the village?
11. Why, do you think, did Native Americans tell this story?
12. What might be another good title for the story?

Creative Time

1. Write the conversation that you think might have occurred between Nekumonta and Shanewis after she woke up from her illness.

2. Draw a map showing Nekumonta's journey as he searched for the healing waters. Include as much detail as you can.

3. Write a rap song encouraging people to be respectful and kind to animals.

Puzzle Time

Find the Native American tribes in the wordsearch.

- Apache
- Blackfoot
- Cherokee
- Cheyenne
- Chippewa
- Choctaw
- Comanche
- Iroquois
- Sioux

```
Q H C H I P P E W A E I O W V
N J G A Y K Z A W D B H Q D W
J V L G J F E Q Y B S U H M Y
X J R F Y G C L D I G E O J C
C O M A N C H E O F F N Q H E
I T Z Z I Z P U U S U S O H Q
D S R K N W Q U V X S C C C C
S E K Q Q O K S I I T A F Y Z
Y E P C R S V Q O A P N D T P
J K B I H F K U W A U K D K B
Z O Y W Q G X L I Y O L M R K
V R O L T B L A C K F O O T G
S E B V M Y T L A Z W S Y T R
O H J E N N E Y E H C F G L A
G C G Y S B F M M Q H K S B A
```

Time Detective

Choose one Native American tribe and research it in detail. Present five interesting facts about the tribe to your class.

Web Watch!
http://www.native-languages.org/kids.htm

http://www.42explore2.com/native4.htm

http://www.mainlesson.com/display.php?author=olcott&book=indian&story=hidden

Integration Project

The Healing Waters

English
Play the word scramble game. Unscramble the words to complete the sentences at http://www.epa.gov/OGWDW/kids/grades_4-8_word_scramble.html

Gaeilge
An bhfuil aon áit slánaithe i do cheantar? Déan tionscnamh faoin áit sin. Cuir pictiúir isteach freisin.

Mathematics
Brainbuster: You have a 5 litre jug, a 3 litre jug and a bowl. How would you fill the bowl with 4 litres using only the two jugs?

Creative writing
Imagine that you could talk to animals. What animal would you talk to? What would you ask it? What would you talk about? Write the conversation.

Geography
Investigate flooding in your locality. Are there any areas that are prone to flooding? What damage has been done in the past? What measures have been taken to combat flooding?

Drama
Conscience Alley: The class form two lines facing each other. As the teacher walks down the line, each child gives advice to Nekumonta. One side gives positive advice to encourage him. The other side reminds him of the dangers and gives negative advice.

Art
Rainsticks were used by Native Americans to call on the spirits to send rain. Make a rainstick. Get a cardboard kitchen roll. Fill it with peas. Tape the ends closed with a large circle. Decorate it with paint.

Science
Do you know how much water you use daily? Try matching each activity to how much water it uses on http://www.epa.gov/OGWDW/kids/flash/flash_matching.html

The Maoris 5

950 Kupe discovers New Zealand

1350 The Great Fleet arrives

1642 Abel Tasman, first European discoverer

1769 Captain James Cook maps the islands

1840 The Treaty of Waitangu is signed

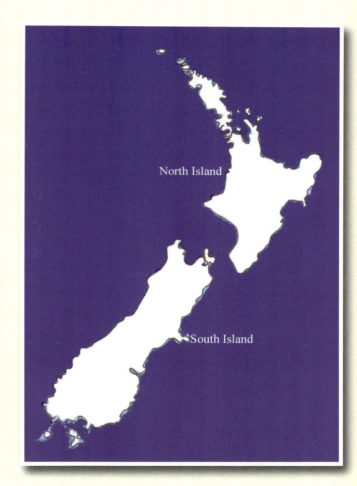

New Zealand is made up of two large islands and several smaller ones. According to Maori legend, the navigator Kupe was the first person to sight New Zealand. He named the country *Aotearoa*, meaning 'The Land of the Long White Cloud'.

The first people to settle in New Zealand were the Maoris. They came from Polynesia. Their history was passed down from generation to generation by word of mouth.

In 1350, the Maoris arrived in a great fleet of canoes, called *waka*. They travelled from their mythical homeland called *Hawaiki*. They brought seeds of plants and sweet potatoes known as *kumara* with them. Dogs and rats also travelled in their canoes.

Many of the first arrivals settled on the east coast of the North Island as the climate was more temperate.

'Kia ora' means 'hello' or 'goodbye' in Maori.

Facts!
15% of the population of New Zealand are of Maori descent.

Children explore aspects of the lives of the Maoris.

Hunters and Fishermen

When the Maoris arrived in New Zealand, they fished and hunted for food. There were many forests on the islands. Birds such as the moa, swan, goose and Giant Haast's eagle were found there. The moa was a flightless bird. The giant moa reached four metres in height and weighed 250kg. These giant birds soon became extinct after they were hunted extensively. Settlers turned to agriculture and began planting their own food.

Moa

Maori Art

Maori art was mainly in the form of carving and weaving. Maoris used the flax plant to make mats, baskets, clothes and fishing nets. Wood carving was used on weapons, treasure boxes, canoes, tools, houses and other ornaments. Maori chiefs often had their skin tattooed.

Maori Warriors

The Maoris lived in small tribes called *iwi*. The *iwi* often fought wars over land. Maori warriors were fierce in battle. When captured, enemies were eaten and their heads were kept as trophies. Maori warriors used stone, bone and wood to make weapons. They did a war dance called the *Haka* before going into battle. The New Zealand rugby team, the All-Blacks, perform the *Haka* before every match.

Maori chief with tattoos

Haka

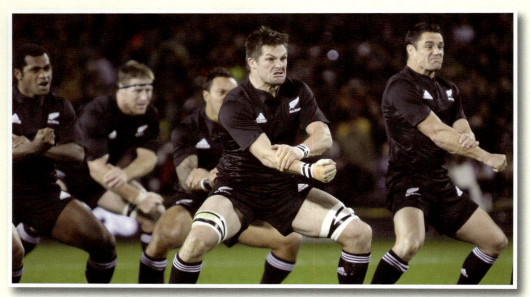

The All-Blacks perform the *Haka*

Abel Tasman

The Dutch explorer Abel Tasman was the first European to reach New Zealand. He sailed along the west coast in 1642. On 13 December, he sighted New Zealand and anchored in Golden Bay five days later. His attempt to land on the island resulted in four of his crew being killed and eaten. Tasman named the islands 'New Zealand'. With the arrival of Captain Cook, more than a century later, the island was finally colonised.

Abel Tasman

First European impression of the Maoris

Word Watch!
Circumnavigate
The word 'circumnavigate' means to 'sail around'.

Captain James Cook

On 6 October 1769, Captain James Cook arrived in New Zealand. He explored and mapped New Zealand. He circumnavigated the two islands aboard his ship Endeavour.

Cook's contact with the Maoris was much friendlier than that of Abel Tasman. One violent incident has been recorded. Cook and his crew tried to trade with some Maoris. However, the Maoris were not interested in working with these strangers. An anxious Cook grew frightened. Believing that the Maoris were about to attack, he quickly opened fire, killing several Maoris.

Captain James Cook

The Marae

Here the chief or *rangatira* speaks to his people on the *marae*. The *marae* is an open space in which the Maoris gather in the centre of the village.

- What, do you think, is the chief saying to his people?
- Describe the clothes worn by the Maoris.
- What, do you think, is hanging in the centre of the *marae*?
- Choose two people who are listening to the chief. Write the conversation they might have had. You could act out this conversation.

Treaty of Waitangi

After the arrival of Captain Cook, many Europeans came and settled in New Zealand. There was much fighting between the settlers and the Maoris. The Treaty of Waitangi was signed in 1840 with the British. The Maoris gave up the right to govern their island in exchange for protection and a guarantee that they could hold on to the land that they already owned.

Question Time

1. Where did the first Maoris come from?
2. Who was the first explorer to discover New Zealand?
3. What does *Aotearoa* mean?
4. How was Maori history recorded?
5. Why did the first arrivals settle on the east coast?
6. Which bird was hunted to extinction by the Maoris?
7. What is the Maori war dance called?
8. Who was the first European to discover New Zealand?
9. How, do you think, did the Maoris feel when the first Europeans arrived?
10. Which explorer first mapped New Zealand?
11. Why, do you think, did the Maoris sign the Treaty of Waitangi?

Creative Time

1. Imagine that you are one of the first Maoris to settle in New Zealand. You have just travelled there in your canoe. Write your diary entries for your journey and arrival in this new and strange land.

2. **Let's Talk!** Imagine that your class are a Maori tribe who have just arrived in *Aotearoa*. A tribal meeting has been called. You must discuss your new homeland.

   Here are some questions for you to consider:

   - How will you survive?
   - Where will you build your homes?
   - What materials will you use to build your home?
   - Where will you find food?
   - What do you think of this new land?
   - What challenges will you face?

Suggest ways in which you can survive and live in this new strange land.

Puzzle Time

Across
3. New Zealand rugby team (3, 6)
5. First European to discover New Zealand (6)
7. Small Maori tribes (3)
8. Giant flightless bird that was hunted to extinction by the Maoris (3)
9. Land of the Long White Cloud (8)
10. Plant used for weaving (4)

Down
1. Nationality of the explorer Abel Tasman (5)
2. Maori chief (9)
4. Sweet potato brought to New Zealand by the Maoris (6)
6. The two islands New Zealand is made up of: North and _____ Island (5)
8. Central gathering place in the Maori village (5)

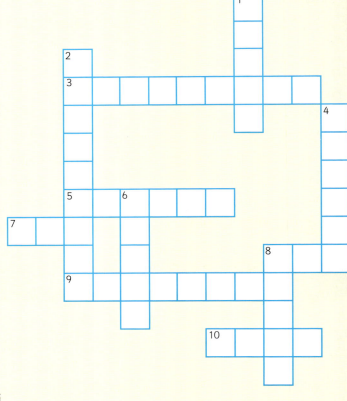

Time Detective

Working as an historian, investigate the history of the Aborigines of Australia. Compare their history to that of the Maoris.

Web Watch!

http://www.maori.org.nz/
http://www.newzealand.com/travel/about-nz/culture/haka-feature/haka.cfm
http://www.aucklandnz.com/

Integration Project

The Maoris

English
Imagine that you are the Dutch explorer Abel Tasman. You have just reached New Zealand. Write a letter home telling of your discovery and the events that followed.

Gaeilge
Déan agallamh i mbeirteanna. Cuireann páiste amháin ceisteanna ar Captain Cook faoina chuid taistil. Tugann an páiste eile na freagraí mar Captain Cook.

Mathematics
Find out what the population of New Zealand is today. If 15% of the population is of Maori descent, find out how many people this is.

Drama
Imagine that your class are a Maori tribe. Hold a meeting to discuss signing the Treaty of Waitangi. Give the pros and cons for signing such a treaty. Organise a vote to find out how many are in favour and how many are against the signing of the treaty.

Geography
Study a map of New Zealand. Make a list of towns and geographical features that have Maori names. Visit:
http://www.teachingonline.org/maori.html

Physical Education
Learn how to perform the *Haka*. To watch the All-Blacks perform the *Haka*, visit:
http://www.allblacks.com/index.cfm?layout=displayNews&newsArticle=2468

Art
Draw a wood carving that could have been used on a Maori canoe. Plan your design first. You could make a clay version of your carving.

Science
The moa bird was hunted to extinction. Scientists learned about this bird from the fossils found in New Zealand. Investigate animals that are in danger of becoming extinct today. What can we do to prevent this?

The Renaissance

Word Watch!
Renaissance
means 'rebirth' and refers to a period of learning and growth in Western Europe from the 15th to the 17th century.

Word Watch!
The Middle Ages
The period before the Renaissance was known as the Middle Ages. During the Middle Ages, learning centred around religion and the church.

The Renaissance began in Northern Italy, in the city of Florence. It spread to Rome and then to the rest of Europe. Italy's long coastline allowed new trade routes to be established. These routes brought new foods and products to Europe as well as ideas from other cultures.

- The Renaissance was a period of great creativity in art and architecture. New ideas were inspired by the study of Ancient Greek and Roman civilisations.
- New developments were made in science, medicine, astronomy and maths.
- People of the Renaissance learned about all aspects of the world, not just about religion.

The ideas and inventions from the Renaissance had a great influence on the modern world. The changes that happened during this time affected the way that we think and live today.

Printing Press

Johann Gutenberg invented the printing press in 1450. Printed information was now more readily available to everyone. Before this, books took a long time to be made because they were written by hand or produced using a hand-carved block method. Books were scarce and only wealthy people could afford to buy them. Now, books could be printed in a few weeks. More people learned to read and they were able to buy books. The printing press helped people to become much more educated.

Johann Gutenberg

Children investigate aspects of the Renaissance and the people who contributed to this period of change.

The Renaissance Men

Leonardo da Vinci and Michelangelo were great artists during the Renaissance. They were called the Renaissance Men because of the contributions they made to this period of history. Renaissance artists made their own paint, tools and materials. In the early days of the Renaissance, they added egg yolk to their paint. This helped to bind the paint and made the painting last for a long time. Later, oil paint was invented.

Patrons were wealthy families who funded the artists. The Medici family was one of these patrons. Artists were sponsored, or paid, by patrons and they produced work that the patrons requested.

Leonardo da Vinci

Leonardo da Vinci was a mathematician, artist, sculptor, engineer and inventor. He drew up early plans for a helicopter, cannon and tank. He is often described as one of the greatest artists of all time. *The Mona Lisa* and *The Last Supper* are some of his most famous works. He loved drawing the human body.

The Mona Lisa

The Mona Lisa is a painting of Lisa del Giocondo. She was the wife of a wealthy silk merchant. Is she smiling in the painting? What do you think?

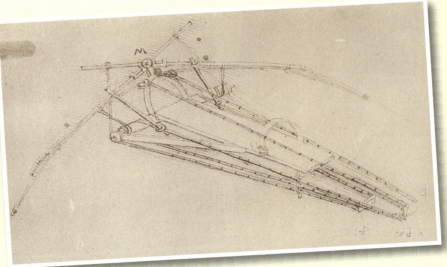

Drawings for a 'flying machine' – helicopter

The Last Supper

Michelangelo

Michelangelo was an artist, sculptor, engineer and poet. He was very interested in the human body. He studied anatomy in order to make sure that he captured the shape and style of the body correctly. *The Statue of David* and the paintings on the ceiling of the Sistine Chapel are among some of his most famous works. He had to lie on his back in order to paint on the ceiling. He also designed the dome of St Peter's Basilica in Rome. Michelangelo worked under the patronage of Lorenzo de Medici. Lorenzo was ruler of Florence until 1492.

Fast Facts!
Damage to *La Pietā*

Michelangelo's famous statue of the Virgin and Child, called *La Pietà*, was damaged throughout the years. Four fingers of the Virgin's left hand were broken when the statue was being moved. These were repaired in 1736. In 1972, a man attacked the statue using a hammer. The statue was repaired and is now kept behind a bullet-proof glass in St Peter's Basilica in Rome.

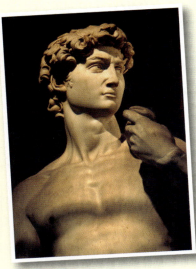

The Statue of David

La Pietà

Roof of Sistine Chapel

St Peter's Basilica in Rome

Timeline of Famous Works

Create a timeline of some of the most famous works of art created during the Renaissance.

Web Watch!
Be a patron of the arts yourself. Visit:
http://www.renaissanceconnection.org/main.cfm
Play the Renaissance Time Machine at
http://www.activehistory.co.uk/Miscellaneous/free_stuff/renaissance/frameset.htm

Renaissance Literature

In the 16th century, books, poems and plays became more widely available. Before this, books were mainly written in Latin. Now, new books appeared written in Italian, English and other languages. *The Prince* by Machiavelli and *Courtier* by Castiglione were two examples of books written in Italian that became very popular. As the Renaissance spread to other countries, the works of William Shakespeare in English also became widely read.

Fast Facts!
Influence of Roman Civilisation
Shakespeare's plays *Julius Caesar*, *Romeo and Juliet* and *Anthony and Cleopatra* were based on stories from Ancient Roman civilisation.

Machiavelli

Question Time

1. What does Renaissance mean?
2. Which civilisations had a great impact on the Renaissance?
3. Where did the Renaissance begin?
4. When did the Renaissance occur?
5. Name some Renaissance writers.
6. Who were the Renaissance Men?
7. List **two** of the works of the Renaissance Men.
8. The opening of new trade routes had a great effect on Italy. Why, do you think, would trade have been easier for Italy?
9. Who invented the printing press?
10. Why, do you think, was the invention of the printing press so important?

Creative Time

Leonardo da Vinci wrote backwards in his journal to keep his thoughts and inventions secret. His journals could be read by holding them up to a mirror. Write a secret message that can only be read by using a mirror.

Puzzle Time

Can you name the artist? Write Michelangelo or Leonardo after each fact.

1. He painted the Sistine Chapel.
2. He drew designs for the first helicopter.
3. He painted *The Mona Lisa*.
4. He created *The Statue of David*.
5. He created *The Last Supper*.
6. He loved drawing the human body.
7. He studied anatomy.
8. He used mirror writing to keep his designs a secret.
9. He painted the Sistine Chapel lying on his back.
10. He created *La Pietà*.

Time Detective

Working as an historian, investigate the period called the Reformation that occurred during the Renaissance. During the 15th and early 16th centuries, there were many problems in the Catholic Church. Many people believed that some church leaders were interested only in making money. Martin Luther led a successful revolt against the Catholic Church. Find out what you can about him.

Integration Project

The Renaissance

English
Write a Curriculum Vitae (CV) for Leonardo da Vinci. Write the CV as if you were da Vinci. Include his place and date of birth, work experience and famous works of art.

Gaeilge
Déan póstaer fógraíochta bunaithe ar an bhfionnachtain nua a chuir Johann Gutenberg ar fáil. Déan cur síos ar an bpreas clódóireachta agus faoi cé chomh tábhachtach is atá sé.

Mathematics
Leonardo Fibonacci was a Renaissance mathematician. He came up with his own number sequence by adding the previous two numbers in the list together. Can you fill in the next five numbers in the sequence?
1, 1, 2, 3, 5, 8, 13, 21, ___, ___, ___, ___, ___.

Drama
One member of the class takes on the role of *The Mona Lisa*. This person must sit on a chair and not smile. Each class member in turn attempts to make her smile. The winner is the person who gets her to smile and then takes her seat.

Geography
Investigate the city of Florence, where the Renaissance began. Plan a trip to visit this city. What sights and museums will you include? Take an interactive tour of the city at
http://www.pbs.org/empires/medici/florence/index.html

Music
Listen to the Renaissance folk tune *Greensleeves*. Discuss the meaning of the words. Investigate the music of other Renaissance musicians such as John Dowland and Josquin Des Pres.

Art
Draw a version of the Sistine Chapel. Like Michelangelo, lie on your back. Tape your sheet of paper to the bottom of your desk. Draw your picture lying down. Remember Michelangelo spent four years lying on his back!

Science
Investigate innovations of the past 600 years and then create your own innovation. Visit:
http://www.renaissanceconnection.org/main.cfm

7 Remembering School

School has changed over the years. Modern technology and other changes have had an impact on education. School in the past was very different from school today. The introduction of computers has affected the way we learn.

In 1938, the School's Folklore Commission asked fifth and sixth class school children in Ireland to collect memories of the past from family and friends. The children did this for homework one night a week. These records are stored in the Irish Folklore Collection at University College Dublin.

Look closely at the photograph of a National School in Co. Monaghan c.1903.

1. What is the name of the school?
2. Describe the clothes worn by the children.
3. Who, do you think, is the school teacher?
4. Who, do you think, is the tall girl on the left?
5. What, do you think, are the children doing in the circle?

Children explore work from the Irish Folklore Collection and investigate schools in the past.

The First Schools

The Penal Laws of the late 1600s forbade Catholics to teach in school. This meant that Catholic teachers had to work in secret schools. In the 1700s and early 1800s, schools were called 'Hedge Schools'. This was because many of the classes took place outdoors, next to hedge-rows. The teacher travelled from village to village, staying in local homes.

The National School system was established in 1831. Children could now go to a local primary school that was funded by the government. The better students were sometimes kept on as monitors. Their job was to help the teacher. As classes were often taught in English, the use of the Irish language was not encouraged. Many children were punished for speaking Irish. Read some memories of school, gathered in 1938, to find out about schools in the past.

Word Watch!
Corporal Punishment

In the past, children were punished if they misbehaved or if they did not do their homework. It was common for teachers to slap the pupils on their hands with willow rods or leather straps. This was called 'corporal punishment'.

> **Old Schools**
>
> There was a hedge school in Barney Mc Adam's field in the town land of Oghill. The school was in an Old Quarry. The Teacher's name was Baldy Fox. The school was held here in the Summer and they had no school during the Winter. The teacher stayed in some of the houses in the neighbourhood. The teacher's pay was gifts from the people. They did not do Irish in the school. They taught English Reading, writing and sums. The children sat on stones and pieces of rock and they wrote on slates with slate pencils.
>
> Written by:- James Barlow,
> Told by:- Toam,
> James Barlow Doohamlet,
> Toam Castleblayney,
> Doohamlet Co Monaghan.

1. Who collected this information?
2. What was his address?
3. Who did he interview?
4. What was the teacher's name?
5. Why, do you think, was there no school in winter?

100

19. 7. '38

Schools — Before the national schools were established the pupils were taught in hedge-schools. Some people called them the poirín. They were situated in a field They were held in the open air. The school-masters used to hold school in farmers houses and they hold school in the hedge schools also The teachers used to spend a term with every child. They used not get any government pay only just whatever the farmers wished. The teachers used to teach Irish, English, Arithmetic, Latin, French, and Grammar. When the teachers began to teach English at first

101

19. 7. '38

Continued

they had but little regard for the Irish. Every child had a block around his neck. For every word of Irish spoken there would be a mark put on the block and in the evening the child would get a slap for each word of Irish spoken. Before the national schools were established the people were very poor.

The children used bring roasted potatoes to school and they were called – Scoláirí na prataí rósta.

Rita Lally
Menlough G. S.

Heard from Mrs Devalley
Aged 91 years Polnabrone

1. Who collected this information?
2. What school did she attend?
3. Who did she interview?
4. How old was the person interviewed?
5. How were children punished for speaking Irish?

Let's Investigate!

Gather information about schools in the past. You could interview your parents, grandparents, elderly neighbours or relatives. Here are some questions to help you to get started.

Travel
- How did you travel to school?
- How far was your home from school?
- What did you wear to school?

The School
- How many children were in your school?
- What teachers did you have?
- Which teacher was your favourite? Why?
- What was your happiest memory of school?

Subjects
- What subjects did you learn?
- What was your favourite subject? Why?
- How long was the school day?

Breaktime
- What did you have for lunch?
- What games did you play in the playground?
- Who did you play with in the yard?

Discipline
- How did the teacher punish children who misbehaved?
- How did the teacher reward children?
- What was your worst memory of school?

Tours
- Where did you go on school tours?

Present your information to the class. Divide your work under different headings such as school building, classroom, games, discipline, subjects and teachers.

Question Time

1. What classes in school collected the folklore?
2. In what year were they collected?
3. Why, do you think, was the folklore collected?
4. Why, do you think, were the schools in the past called hedge schools?
5. How was the school master paid?
6. What did the children write on?
7. Where would you find the folklore collection today?
8. How was school in the past similar to school today?
9. How was school in the past different to school today?

Creative Time

1. Design a school of the future. Draw floor plans for the proposed building. Include drawings of what the school will look like. What rooms will you include? Label your work.

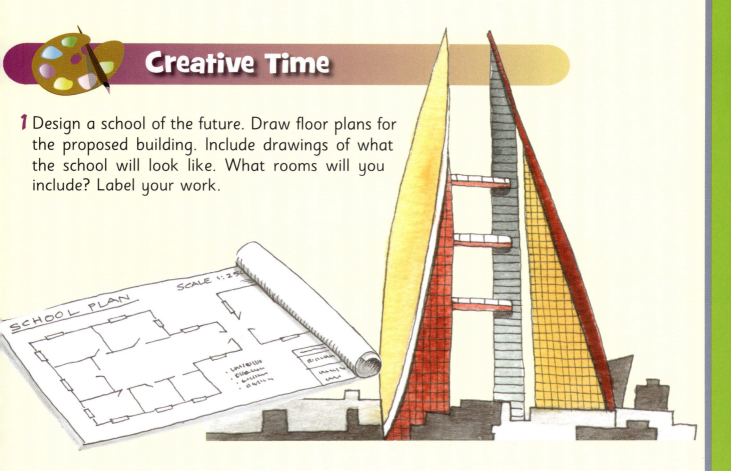

2. Design a statue or a monument that could be erected in your school grounds.
   - Who or what will be honoured by the statue?
   - Is there a historical figure who has influenced your school?
   - Is there someone who has played an important role in your school and deserves to be celebrated?

Puzzle Time

Crossword

Across
2. The schools were often located here (5)
3. The children wrote on these (5)
5. The name schools were given in the past (5)
7. The older student who stayed on to help the teacher (7)

Down
1. The laws that forbade Catholics to teach in school (5)
3. The classes who collected the folklore were fifth and _____ classes (5)
4. The Folklore Collection is located there today (3)
6. How the teacher was paid (5)

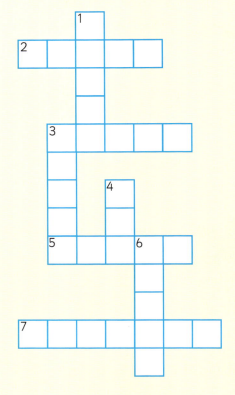

Time Detective

While planting flowers in your school garden, you uncover an old time capsule. Inside you find old letters written by students a hundred years ago. The letters tell all about what each day in school was like, the subjects they learned, what they had for lunch, and where the school was.

Imagine that you were one of these students who lived long ago. Write a letter that was found in the time capsule.

Web Watch!

Visit some school websites at:
http://www.primaryscience.ie/site/activities_school_websites.php

Integration Project

Remembering School

English
Talk for sixty seconds about your first day at school. Who did you sit beside? What activities do you remember? Who was your first teacher? How did you feel?

Gaeilge
Bhí do chara as láthair inniu. Scríobh nóta ag tabhairt treoracha faoin obair bhaile a bhí agat. Cén leathanach agus cén uimhir?

Mathematics
Using a metre stick or trundle wheel, find the area of your classroom, school hall and school yard. Work in pairs. Remember Area = Length x Width.

Drama
Write the front page of a newspaper reporting on the opening of your school. When was it first opened? How many teachers were there? Who was the principal?

Geography
Draw a map of your route to school. Include local landmarks and features. Put a key at the bottom of your map.

Music
Compose a school anthem. Include a school motto and important historical facts about your school.

Art
Design a school flag. What images or symbols would be important to your school? What colours will you choose for the flag?

Science
Design a recycling bin for your school. What shape will it have? How will it encourage people to recycle more? Where should you place it?

8. The Liberator

Childhood

Daniel O'Connell was born near Cahirciveen, Co. Kerry, on 6 August 1775. He was adopted at an early age by his uncle, Maurice O'Connell.

O'Connell was educated in France and London and became a successful barrister. His experiences of the French Revolution left him with a hatred of violence. He felt it was important that peaceful means should be used to gain independence. He was against the risings of 1798 and 1803. He believed that Irish people would have to use politics and not force to achieve their aims.

Statue of Daniel O'Connell, 1900

> 'Not for all the universe contains, would I, in the struggle for what I conceive to be my country's cause, consent to the effusion of a single drop of human blood, except my own.'
>
> 28 February 1843

In 1802, O'Connell married Mary O'Connell and they had twelve children, six boys and six girls. Sadly, only seven of the children survived (four sons and three daughters). His four sons later became Members of Parliament.

Children investigate the life of Daniel O'Connell and his contribution to Catholic Emancipation.

Catholic Emancipation

Daniel O'Connell set up the Catholic Association in 1823. Members paid a penny a month for membership. This became known as 'Catholic rent'. The goal of the association was Catholic Emancipation, that is, the right for Irish Catholics to become members of parliament. The association collected funds which were used to support a political campaign. Thousands of people took part in peaceful protests. The Catholic Church supported the association.

In 1828, O'Connell was elected as a Member of Parliament (MP) for Co. Clare. He won by a majority of 1,075 votes, 2,057 votes to 982. At this time, voting took place in public. Tenants were often told who to vote for by their landlord. If they did not vote for the landlord's choice, they could be evicted. This made O'Connell's success even greater. He could not take up his seat in Westminster as Catholics were not allowed to sit in the British Parliament at this time.

The British government feared a rising and so allowed Catholic Emancipation to become law in 1829. O'Connell gave up his successful law career and dedicated himself to politics. Finally, in 1830, he was able to take his seat in the House of Commons.

> **Word Watch!**
> **Duel**
>
> Sometimes, people settled arguments by having a duel. This involved two people shooting at each other with pistols.
>
> In 1815, O'Connell called the Dublin Corporation a 'beggarly corporation'. A man named D'Esterre, who was a member of the Corporation, believed that this was a terrible insult.
>
> He challenged O'Connell to a duel. Even though O'Connell was against violence, he accepted the challenge. D'Esterre was killed. O'Connell was upset by his death and he paid money to D'Esterre's family for many years to help to support them.

The Repeal Association

Although O'Connell had enjoyed huge success and was now known as The Liberator, he still was not satisfied. He wanted to have the Act of Union of 1800 repealed (cancelled). Under the Act of Union, there was no government in Dublin. Irish Members of Parliament had to travel to Westminster, London. O'Connell was determined to get an Irish parliament for Ireland. This was his ultimate goal. He set up the Repeal Association for this cause.

Monster Meetings

O'Connell was elected Lord Mayor of Dublin in 1841. He was the first Catholic to hold this post since 1690. O'Connell was a great speaker. He began organising large meetings throughout Ireland. In 1843, he organised thirty-one such meetings. These meetings became known as 'Monster Meetings' as they drew enormous crowds. One meeting held at Tara on 15 August 1843 was attended by over 750,000 people.

The British government was becoming more alarmed at the strength of the repeal movement. On 8 October 1843, the British Prime Minister banned a Monster Meeting which had been organised to take place in Clontarf. O'Connell feared that there might be violence or bloodshed, so he agreed to cancel the meeting. Despite this, he was arrested on 30 May 1844 and he spent three months in jail.

Choose two people from the picture attending the Monster Meeting at Tara. Write the conversation you think they might be having.
Act out the conversation with a partner.

Meeting Cancelled

NOTICE.

WHEREAS, there has appeared, under the Signatures of "E. B. Sugden, C., Donoughmore, Eliot, F. Blackburne, E. Blakeney, Fred. Shaw, T. B. C. Smith," a paper being, or purporting to be, a PROCLAMATION, drawn up in very loose and inaccurate terms, and manifestly misrepresenting known facts; the objects of which appear to be, to prevent the PUBLIC MEETING, intended to be held TO-MORROW, the 8th instant, at CLONTARF, *to petition Parliament* for the REPEAL of the baleful and destructive measure of the LEGISLATIVE UNION.

AND WHEREAS, such Proclamation has not appeared until *late in the Afternoon of this Saturday, the 7th*, so that it is utterly impossible that the knowledge of its existence could be communicated in the usual Official Channels, or by the Post, in time to have its contents known to the Persons intending to meet at CLONTARF, for the purpose of Petitioning, as aforesaid, whereby ill-disposed Persons may have an opportunity, under cover of said Proclamation, to provoke Breaches of the Peace, or to commit Violence on Persons intending to proceed peaceably and legally to the said Meeting.

WE, therefore, the COMMITTEE of the LOYAL NATIONAL REPEAL ASSOCIATION, do most earnestly request and entreat, that all well-disposed persons will, IMMEDIATELY on receiving this intimation, repair to their own dwellings, and not place themselves in peril of any collision, or of receiving any ill-treatment whatsoever.

And We do further inform all such persons, that without yielding in any thing to the unfounded allegations in said alleged Proclamation, we deem it prudent and wise, and above all things humane, to DECLARE that said

Meeting is abandoned, and is not to be held.

Signed by Order,

DANIEL O'CONNELL,
Chairman of the Committee.

T. M. RAY, Secretary.

Saturday, 7th October, 1843.
3 o'Clock P. M.

RESOLVED—That the above Cautionary Notice be immediately transmitted by Express to the Very Reverend and Reverend Gentlemen who signed the Requisition for the CLONTARF MEETING, and to all adjacent Districts, SO AS TO PREVENT the influx of Persons coming to the intended Meeting.

GOD SAVE THE QUEEN.

Browne, Printer, 36, Nassau-street.

Study the notice issued by Daniel O'Connell cancelling the Clontarf meeting. Answer the following questions:
1. Describe the emblem at the top of the notice.
2. What does the notice advise people to do?
3. Why, do you think, was the notice not issued until late in the afternoon?
4. Who was the Secretary of the Committee?
5. Why, do you think, did O'Connell end the notice with 'God Save the Queen'?

Death of O'Connell

When O'Connell was released from jail, he continued with his campaign to repeal the Act of Union. However, the energy and fight had gone out of the organisation. The failure of the potato crop in 1845 and the famine that followed were more important issues than the question of repeal.

By this time, O'Connell was seventy years old and his health was failing. In March 1847, he set out for Italy. He died in Genoa on 15 May. At his request, his heart was sent to Rome, while his body was buried in Glasnevin Cemetery, Dublin.

O'Connell Remembered

O'Connell successfully achieved Catholic Emancipation. After the establishment of the Irish Free State, his statue was erected on the main street in Dublin, Sackville Street. This street was renamed O'Connell Street in his honour. Other streets in Limerick, Ennis, Sligo and Clonmel are also named in his memory.

O'Connell monument, Ennis, Co. Clare

O'Connell Street, Limerick

Old 20 pound note showing Daniel O'Connell

Question Time

1. Where was Daniel O'Connell born?
2. Why, do you think, might Daniel O'Connell have been educated abroad?
3. Why was O'Connell opposed to violence as a means of achieving independence?
4. Why was the Catholic Association set up?
5. What was 'Catholic rent'?
6. When was Catholic Emancipation finally granted?
7. Why, do you think, was Daniel O'Connell called 'The Liberator'?
8. Why, do you think, were the meetings of 1843 called 'Monster Meetings'?
9. Why did O'Connell cancel the Monster Meeting planned for Clontarf?
10. Where did O'Connell die?

Creative Time

1. Imagine that you were at the Monster Meeting in Tara. Write about your experience of the meeting. Describe the scene. How did the crowd react to O'Connell's speech? How did his words make you feel?
2. An epitaph is an inscription on a tombstone in memory of the person buried there. Write an epitaph that might have been placed on Daniel O'Connell's headstone.
   What were his greatest achievements?
   How will he be remembered?
3. Imagine that you are a journalist working for a newspaper. Write the article that might have been included under the following headline published after O'Connell's death:

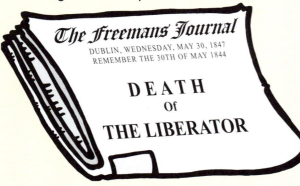

- Why did it take so long for O'Connell's death to be announced?
- What happened on 30 May 1844? Why, do you think, is this mentioned?

Puzzle Time

Fill in the correct words in the blank spaces.

Daniel O'Connell was born near _____, County Kerry. He was educated abroad in _____ and _____. His experiences of the _____ _____ left him with a hatred of _____. He believed that _____ methods should be used. He worked as a _____ for several years before being elected as MP for County _____ in 1828.

In 1823 he helped to set up the _____ _____. Its goal was _____ _____. Members paid a fee of one _____ a month. This money was used to fund the organisation. O'Connell was successful and Catholic Emancipation became law in _____.

O'Connell then turned his attention to repeal the _____ __ _____. In 1843, he organised Monster Meetings throughout Ireland. The largest of these meetings was held in _____ and it was attended by 750,000 people. The British Government banned a meeting organised to take place in _____, Co. Dublin. O'Connell cancelled the meeting to avoid any violence or bloodshed. His supporters were disappointed. O'Connell died in Genoa in _____.

Time Detective

Create a timeline for the life of Daniel O'Connell. Write a label on the dates marked, showing the key events in his life.

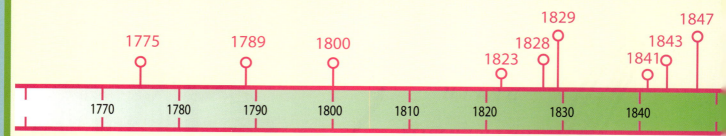

Web Watch!

http://multitext.ucc.ie/d/Daniel_OConnell

Integration Project

English
You have been chosen to speak at one of O'Connell's Monster Meetings. Write the speech that you would give, convincing the people of the importance of peaceful protest.

Gaeilge
Is tusa Daniel O'Connell. Tá tú istigh sa phríosún. Scríobh litir chuig do chlann faoi do chuid ama istigh. Cad a dhéanfaidh tú nuair a scaoilfear amach tú?

Mathematics
O'Connell Street in Dublin is one of Europe's widest streets. It measures 500 metres in length and 46 metres in width at the southern end and 49 metres in width at the northern end. If the average width is 47.5m, what is the area of O'Connell Street?

Drama
Hot Seat: One member of your class takes on the role of Daniel O'Connell and sits in the 'Hot Seat'. Take it in turns to ask him questions about his life.

The Liberator

Geography
O'Connell went to school at St Omer and Douai in France. Investigate schools in France. What subjects do they learn? How do schools in France compare to schools in Ireland?

SPHE
Catholic Emancipation became law in 1829. Explore inequality and discrimination in Ireland today. How could this be addressed? Consider homelessness, poverty, prejudice and stereotyping.

Art
Imagine that it is the year 1843 and a Monster Meeting is being held in your locality. O'Connell is due to attend the meeting. Design a poster to advertise the event.

Science
When O'Connell died, his heart was sent to Rome. Find out five interesting facts about your heart. Share your information with your class.

9 Planes, Trains and Automobiles

Inventions in transport have changed our everyday life. Travel has become faster, more comfortable and cheaper. Each development makes travelling much easier. The development of the wheel was an important invention. Imagine what life would be like without the wheel. Think about how much we depend on buses, cars, bicycles, and aeroplanes!

Bicycles

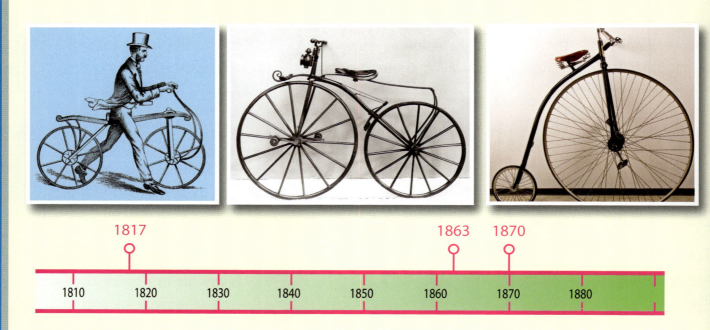

1817
Baron Drais Von Suaerbronn invented the **hobby-horse** bicycle. The riders rolled themselves along by walking their feet on the ground.

1863
The **boneshaker** was invented by **Pierre Michaux**. It was a two-wheeled bicycle made of wood. It also had pedals.

1870
The first all-metal bicycle was invented by **James Starley**. Called the **Penny farthing,** it had a large front wheel and a small rear wheel.

Children investigate developments in transport through a line of development study.

Trains

The invention of trains transformed industry and how people travelled. Travel became faster and more comfortable. Horse-drawn carriages were replaced with steam engines.

1804 — 1814 — 1834

| 1805 | 1810 | 1815 | 1820 | 1825 | 1830 | 1835 | 1840 |

1804
Richard Trevithick invented the first steam-powered tram locomotive. It hauled ten tons of iron, seventy men and five extra wagons.

1814
In 1814, **George Stephenson** invented his first locomotive. In 1829, he invented *The Rocket* locomotive. With an average speed of 20km per hour, this locomotive won the top prize of £500 in a competition called The Rainhill Trials!

1834
The first railway in Ireland ran from Dublin to Kingstown, now Dún Laoghaire. The line was 10km long and cost over £300,000 to build.

Steam-powered locomotives developed rapidly after the success of Stephenson's *Rocket*. Soon, many countries began to develop their own railways. For over a hundred years, the steam train was the most common form of transport. In the 1950s, steam trains were replaced with diesel and electric trains. In 1984, the Dublin Area Rapid Transit, DART, was opened. The light rail system, Luas, began operating in Dublin in 2004. The Luas Green line from St Stephen's Green to Sandyford runs along some of the old Harcourt Street tram line.

Automobiles

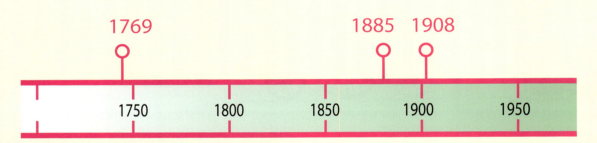

1769
Nicholas Cugnot, a French inventor, designed the first steam-powered tricycle. There was a huge boiler at the front. Its top speed was 3km per hour.

1885
German engineer **Karl Benz** invented the *motorwagen*, the first motor-powered tricycle. Its top speed was 13km per hour.

1908
Henry Ford's Model T Ford was one of the most popular cars. By mass-producing this car, he made it more affordable. Its top speed was 65km per hour

The development of the automobile from steam powered to motor powered has had a huge influence on our lives. The first motor cars were started by turning a starting handle at the front of the car. This was quite difficult and often dangerous. Many people broke their arms trying to start their cars. The first cars were open-topped. Drivers were often hit by loose stones, mud and dust. Soon, better roads were built.

Fast Facts!
The Red Flag Act of 1865 meant that a person had to walk 50 metres in front of a car, carrying a red flag to signal to the driver when to stop.

Planes

For centuries, people dreamed of flying. Leonardo da Vinci made one of the first drawings for a flying machine in the 1480s. From the first hot-air balloon flight in 1783 to the Wright brothers' first successful flight in 1903, the pioneers of flying were brave and daring.

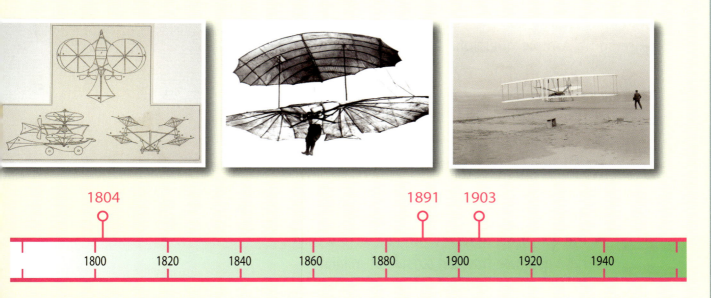

1804
Sir George Cayley is known as the 'Father of Flight'. He built a glider that carried his gardener several feet.

1891
German engineer **Otto Lilienthal** designed a glider that could fly carrying a person. He was later killed in a glider accident.

1903
The Wright Brothers made their first successful flight on 17 December 1903, at Kitty Hawk, USA. This historic flight lasted 12 seconds.

Orville and Wilbur Wright's flight soon led to an increased interest in flying. Daring pilots tried to stay in the air longer and to travel long distances. Frenchman Louis Blériot was the first person to fly across the English Channel, in 1909. In 1919, John Alcock and Arthur Brown were the first pilots to fly non-stop across the Atlantic Ocean. Despite bad weather, radio failure, and ice on the wings, they landed successfully in Ireland.

Charles Lindbergh was the first to fly solo across the Atlantic, in 1927. The flight from New York to Paris took him 33½ hours. His greatest challenge was to stay awake for so long!

Meanwhile, women were also setting new records. Amelia Earhart was the first woman to fly solo across the Atlantic, in 1932.

Travel over the Generations

Investigate how your family travelled in the past. Interview a parent or grandparent. Ask yourself the same questions. Compare their answers with yours.

- How has travel changed over the years?
- How have developments in transport affected your life?

Here are some sample questions to help get you started:

- How did you travel to school?
- How did you travel to visit your friends?
- List the different methods of transport that you have used over the years.
- Where did you go on holidays when you were young?
- Did you travel abroad when you were a child?
- Have you ever travelled outside of Ireland?
- Have you ever travelled outside of Europe?
- How many times were you on a plane as a child?
- What was your favourite method of transport?
- Did you have a family car? What model was it?

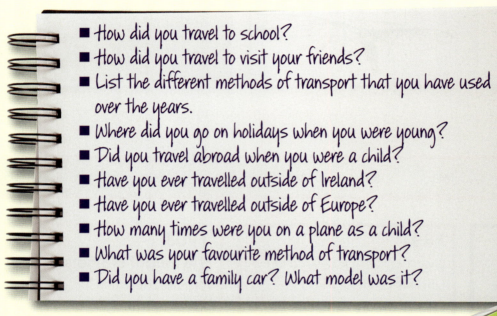

The story of developments in transport still continues.
- What new developments will the future hold?
- How will the transport of the future be powered?
- Will solar panels be used?
- Will recycled materials be used?
- How can we make travel more environmentally friendly?

The way people travel affects our climate. Cars, aeroplanes, buses and ships need oil for their engines. Burning oil has caused the earth's climate to warm up. This is called global warming.

In recent times, transport is being developed which is environmentally friendly. Can developments in technology lead to vehicles that have no harmful emissions?

Web Watch!

To calculate how much carbon your family produces, visit: http://www.carbonfootprint.com/calculator.aspx

Question Time

1. List **ten** different methods of transport.
2. Why, do you think, was the boneshaker given that name?
3. Who invented 'The Rocket'?
4. Where was the first railway line in Ireland?
5. Who invented the first steam-powered tricycle?
6. How did Henry Ford make his cars affordable?
7. Who is often called the 'Father of Flight'?
8. How was Otto Lilienthal killed?
9. Where was the first successful flight?
10. What difficulties did Alcock and Brown face on their Atlantic flight?
11. What does the term 'carbon footprint' mean?

Creative Time

1. Imagine that you are Karl Benz. Design a poster to advertise the *motorwagen*. What will attract people to buy this car?
   What are the key selling points? Include an interesting title and a picture of the car.
2. In 1815, Charles Bianconi started the first horse-car service in Ireland. Look at the photograph and answer the following questions:

(a) In your opinion, which seat would be the cheapest seat?
(b) Why, do you think, were these cars called 'Bians'?
(c) Imagine that you are one of the passengers on the horse car. Write about your journey. Mention the sights, sounds and smells that you experienced on the journey.

Puzzle Time

Unscramble the following methods of transport:

1. usaL _____
2. mart _____
3. tho ria loblano _____
4. digler _____
5. arc _____
6. traD _____
7. pearalone _____
8. cipholeret _____
9. libeycc _____
10. chaty _____
11. sesbu _____

Time Detective

Imagine that it is the year 3010 and you are an archaeologist working on a dig. You have just uncovered an historic artefact. It is a car from the year 2010.

- What make or model of car have you uncovered?
- How is the car powered?
- What developments have happened over the years in automobile technology?

Present a report on your findings to your class.
Include images of this historical artefact.

Web Watch!
http://www.cie.ie/about_us/schools_and_enthusiasts.asp#1
http://www.cybersteering.com/trimain/history/ecars.html
http://www.century-of-flight.net/
http://www.discoverychannel.co.uk/cars/timeline/

Integration Project

Planes, Trains and Automobiles

English
Create an A to Z booklet on transport. Try to think of one form of transport for as many letters of the alphabet as you can.

Gaeilge
Déanann páiste pictiúr de mhodh iompair ar an gclár bán. Tá ar na páistí eile ainm a chur air. Déanann an páiste leis an bhfreagra ceart an chéad phictiúr eile.

Mathematics
If a car travelled 235km in two and a half hours, what speed was it travelling at, per hour? How far would it have travelled in five hours?

Drama
Working in pairs, act out the conversation between two people on a bus. Take on the role of different characters. What questions will you ask?

Geography
Choose four methods of transport to get home from different locations around the world. Choose the shortest route, listing all the methods of transport used.

SPHE
Design a poster encouraging younger children to obey the Safe Cross Code. The aim of the poster is to make them think about travelling to school safely. How will you catch their attention?

Art
Design a method of transport of the future. How will it be powered? What new inventions will be used? Label the different parts, explaining how it works.

Science
Make a bridge using a sheet of paper and two blocks. Investigate ways of making your bridge stronger. Try folding your paper like a fan. Alter the distance between the blocks. Does this make your bridge stronger? Test your structure, seeing how many coins it can hold.

10 World War I

World War I lasted for four years, from 1914 to 1918, and involved many different countries. It began in Europe but soon other countries around the world were involved.

On 28 June 1914, Archduke Franz Ferdinand, the heir to the Austrian throne, was assassinated by a Serbian nationalist. The Austrians blamed Serbia for the assassination and declared war on them on 28 July. Within a week, Russia, Germany and France joined in the fighting.

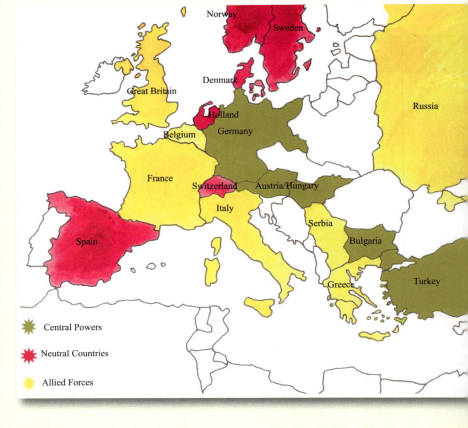

World War I was known as the Great War. It was fought between two sides, the **Allied Forces** and the **Central Powers**. Britain, France, Russia and Italy made up the Allied Forces. Germany, Austria-Hungary, Turkey and Bulgaria made up the Central Powers. Both sides expected that the war would be over by Christmas. However, new inventions in warfare meant that this war would last for a very long time.

On 4 August, Germany invaded neutral Belgium on its way to France. Britain entered the war to protect France. Germany fought a war on two fronts, France to the west and Russia to the east. It had hoped to defeat France quickly before turning its effort to the eastern front. Millions of soldiers died in battles such as the Battle of Verdun and the Battle of the Somme.

Children examine aspects of life during World War I and investigate evidence from this period.

Trench Warfare

World War I brought a new type of warfare known as trench warfare. Soldiers dug trenches surrounded by barbed wire to protect themselves. By the spring of 1915, trenches were filled with millions of soldiers. The two sides were separated by an area known as 'No Man's Land'. Soldiers lay in the trenches fearing mustard and tear gas, gunfire, lice, large rats and diseases. Dead bodies were left to rot in the trenches. These attracted rats which sometimes grew to the size of small dogs! Read one soldier's memories of the dreaded trenches.

Every morning before dawn, we were woken from our sleep and ordered to guard against a dawn raid by the enemy. Yet another day had begun. As I stood there with my bayonet in my hand, I knew the enemy were probably doing the exact same thing as us. Then we'd fire into the distant mist reminding them we were still here!

The mornings were always busy. Before breakfast, we had to clean our rifles and equipment before the officer's inspection. After breakfast, we were given our daily chores. I always hoped to get the easier chores like refilling the sandbags or repairing the trench. No one liked the cleaning of the toilet!

The days seemed to pass so slowly. It seemed they would never end. We were hardly allowed move until nightfall for fear of gunfire. We'd write letters home or try to catch some much needed sleep! There was plenty of time to think of home. We'd try to grab some food where possible. I'll never forget the terrible smell of the trenches. The smell of bodies left to rot. The smell of rats and dried sweat. You never got used to those smells.

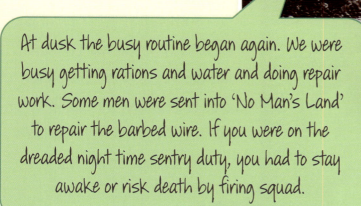

At dusk the busy routine began again. We were busy getting rations and water and doing repair work. Some men were sent into 'No Man's Land' to repair the barbed wire. If you were on the dreaded night time sentry duty, you had to stay awake or risk death by firing squad.

Women and World War I

Before the war, there were not very many jobs available to women. This changed suddenly when World War I began. The men were sent off to fight in the war and women were required to do the jobs done previously by men.

Some women also went to war. They worked as nurses to help the injured soldiers. However, the majority of women had to stay at home. They played an important part in the war effort. Some women worked in the munitions factories producing weapons and shells for the war. Others worked in public transport, on the telephone exchanges or as labourers on the farms.

After the war, women in Britain and America were given the vote in recognition of the role they played during the Great War.

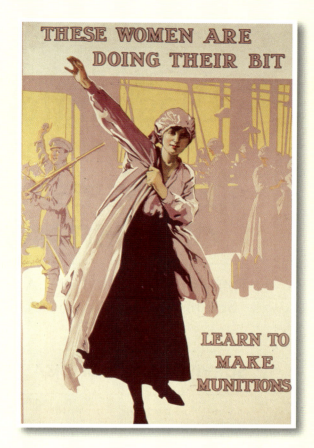

Women working in the munitions factories

The luxury ship the *Lusitania* was sailing from New York to Liverpool. On 7 May 1915, the Germans sank the *Lusitania* off the coast of Ireland. 1,198 passengers and crew lost their lives as a result.

Washington County News
13 May 1915

1,200 PERISHED ON LUSITANIA

SMEAR OF FLOTSAM ON FACE OF SEA MARKS GRAVE OF SUNKEN STEAMER.

SURVIVORS TELL OF DISASTER

One Hundred and Forty-nine of 1200 Who Perished Lie in Improvised Morgue at Queenstown.

London. — Dispatch to the Exchange Telegraph Company from Liverpool says the official list of survivors of the Lusitania includes the names of 487 passengers and 274 crew.

Queenstown. — A smear of flotsam on the face of a calm sea 23 miles from this port marks the grave of the Cunarder Lusitania, victim of a German submarine.

One hundred and forty-nine of the 1200 persons who perished with the liner lie in improvised morgues in old buildings that line the Queenstown harbor. They either were picked up dead or succumbed after landing.

The 645 survivors of the disaster here are quartered in hotels, residences and hospitals, some too badly hurt to be moved. Two groups left here clad in misfit clothing for Dublin by rail and thence by boat to Holy Head. The injuries of some are so serious that additional deaths are expected and nearly all are too dazed to understand fully what happened.

The survivors do not agree as to whether the submarine fired one or two torpedoes. A few say they saw the periscope and many attest to tracing the wake of the foam as a projectile raced toward the vessel.

The only points in which all concur is that the torpedo struck the vessel a vital blow amidships, causing her to list almost immediately to the starboard. In this careening fashion she plowed forward some distance smashing the left boat's davits as she did so and making the launching of boats well nigh impossible until headway had been ceasued. How far the Lusitania struggled forward after being struck and how long it was before she disappeared beneath the waves are points on which few passengers agree, estimates of the time she remained afloat ranging from 8 to 20 minutes. The list to starboard so elevated life boats on the port side as to render them useless and it is said only two on that side were launched.

1. How many people died as a result of the sinking of the *Lusitania*?
2. How many passengers were on the ship?
3. Why are the survivors unsure whether one or two torpedoes were fired?
4. Why were the people on the ship unable to use all of the lifeboats?
5. Do you think propaganda was used in this article?
6. Why, do you think, did it take so long for the sinking to be reported?

Peace at Last

By early November 1918, Germany was the only Central Power left fighting in the war. On 7 November, a German delegation crossed the front line, in France, to discuss peace terms. A peace treaty, 'The Treaty of Versailles', was signed. Germany was forced to pay huge damages to the Allied forces. Germany also lost land and had its army size limited.

European leaders after signing The Treaty of Versailles

The Outcome of the War

World War I finally ended on the eleventh hour of the eleventh day of the eleventh month of 1918. It had been the worst disaster in history. Over 21 million people had died and large parts of Europe lay devastated. Soldiers returned home unable to forget the horrors of war. Almost 210,000 Irishmen fought in World War I. They served in the British forces. 35,000 Irishmen are believed to have died during the war.

Celebrating the end of the war

Question Time

1. In which year did World War I begin?
2. Why, do you think, was the war called 'The Great War'?
3. What countries were known as the Allied Forces?
4. What countries were known as the Central Powers?
5. List some European countries that were neutral.
6. What was life like for soldiers in the trenches?
7. What was the land between the trenches known as?
8. Why were more jobs available to women during the war?
9. Why, do you think, did the Germans sink the *Lusitania*?
10. On what date did World War I end?
11. Why, do you think, were there more casualties than in any previous war?

Creative Time

1. **War Poetry.** World War I inspired writers and poets. Many of them had been soldiers and they wrote about their experiences of war. Read the following extract from a war poem written by Wilfred Owen and answer the questions that follow.

The Show
by Wilfred Owen

My soul looked down from a vague height, with Death,
As unremembering how I rose or why,
And saw a sad land, weak with sweats of dearth,
Gray, cratered like the moon with hollow woe,
And pitted with great pocks and scabs of plagues.

Across its beard, that horror of harsh wire,
There moved thin caterpillars, slowly uncoiled.
It seemed they pushed themselves to be as plugs
Of ditches, where they writhed and shrivelled, killed.

- What do the following words mean: dearth, pocks, plagues, writhed?
- Why are the men compared to 'thin caterpillars'?
- Why, do you think, were the soldiers described as 'plugs'?

2 Imagine that you are a soldier stationed in the trenches during the war. Write a letter home telling your family about your daily routine, your news and your hopes for the future.

3 Governments used propaganda posters to persuade women to work. Design a wartime poster encouraging women to work on the home front. What catchy slogan and image will you use to convince them to go out to work?

Puzzle Time

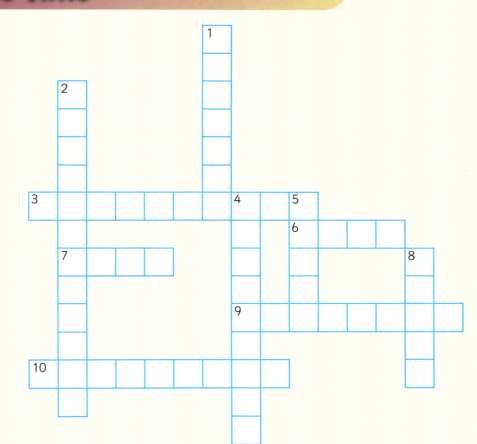

Across

3 The peace treaty that was signed – The Treaty of _____ (10)
6 A British war poet who wrote *The Show*. (4)
7 How many years the war lasted. (4)
9 A network of ditches dug to protect soldiers. (8)
10 The Archduke who was assassinated in 1914. (9)

Down

1 Countries that did not take sides in the war (7)
2 Britain, France, Russia and Italy were known as the _____ _____ (6,6)
4 The luxury ship that was sunk by the Germans (9)
5 This battle was one of the bloodiest battles of World War I – Battle of the S_____ (5)
8 World War I was known as the '_____ War' (5)

2

What is the message of these wartime posters?

Time Detective

Create a timeline of key events that happened in World War I. Here are some important events to include:

- Assassination of Archduke Ferdinand
- Sinking of the *Lusitania*
- Battle of Verdun
- Battle of the Somme
- United States declares war on Germany
- Signing of the Versailles Treaty

Web Watch!

Play a game to defend your trench. Visit:
http://www.bbc.co.uk/schools/worldwarone/hq/trenchwarfare.shtml
Explore the dangers of trench warfare at
http://www.warmuseum.ca/cwm/games/overtop/index_e.html

Integration Project

World War I

English
Write your own war poem. Use images to create a visual picture of war. Read poems by war poets such as Edgar Guest, Wilfred Owen and Francis Ledwidge to inspire you.

Gaeilge
Tráth na gceisteanna: I ngrúpaí, scríobh ceisteanna bunaithe ar an gCogadh Mór. Cuir na ceisteanna ar na grúpaí eile. Faigheann tú pointí muna bhfuil an freagra ceart acu.

Mathematics
In pairs, play the card game War. Each pair has a deck of cards. The cards are split in two and placed face down. The two players turn over a card at the same time. Each card is worth its face value. To win the cards, you multiply the two numbers together. The first person to call out the correct answer wins the cards.

Drama
Each member of the class takes on the role of a person from a different country in World War I. Give your views about the war and say how it affects your country.

Geography
Using a blank map, mark in the location of some of the important battles of World War I. Where did most of the fighting occur?

Music
To listen to war songs such as 'It's a long way to Tipperary' and 'Pack up your troubles', visit:
http://www.bbc.co.uk/schools/worldwarone/observer/

Art
Design a poster on the theme of peace. What will your motto be? What symbols or images will you include?

Science
Many soldiers died or were injured in gas attacks during World War I. Mustard gas was the most deadly gas used. It was odourless and needed twelve hours to take effect. Investigate the effects of mustard gas.

11 The Emergency

World War II began on 1 September 1939, when Germany invaded Poland. Over the next six years, the war was fought between the **Allies** of Britain, France, America and Russia and the **Axis powers** of Germany, Italy and Japan.

Éamon De Valera was the Taoiseach of Ireland at the time and he called this period 'The Emergency'. Ireland declared itself to be neutral (not taking sides) and passed an Emergency Act giving the government new powers such as censorship of communication and the control of movement in the sea and air. Ireland's neutrality highlighted its independence from Britain. Sweden and Switzerland also remained neutral during World War II.

Éamon De Valera

Other Neutral Countries

Denmark, Norway, Holland and Belgium were neutral at the beginning of the war. However, they were invaded by the German army. Many Irish people were fearful of an invasion by the Germans or British.

Irish people experienced some hardships during the war but these were nothing compared to the experiences of those involved in the war.

Neutral Countries in World War II

Children explore aspects of life in Ireland during World War II and examine evidence from this period.

Artefacts of the Emergency

Censorship was introduced from the start of the Emergency. Censorship meant people could not comment about the war or take sides in newspapers, books or films. As a result, Irish people were often unaware of what was going on in Europe.

Gas masks were distributed to the people to protect them from poisonous gases. Gas masks worked by allowing clean air to be taken in. They also filtered out the poisoned air.

Using one of these artefacts, tell the story of a person who used it during the Emergency in Ireland.

Rationing

Food had to be rationed during the war. There were shortages of imported foods such as sugar, tea and flour. Fruit such as bananas and oranges were not available. Meat, clothes and chocolate were rationed. In 1942, bread was also rationed.

People were given ration books and allowed only a certain amount of these items each month. Ration books were small booklets with coupons for different food. People found it hard to live on these rations. Consider what it was like to have only 14g of tea, 225g of sugar and 170g of butter every week!

The Department of Agriculture encouraged people to grow vegetables during the Emergency. Study this leaflet carefully and answer the following questions.

1. Why did the government want people to grow their own food?
2. Why should people choose to grow potatoes?
3. Who issued this leaflet?
4. Why, do you think, was this leaflet issued?

Transport

During the Emergency years, there were also fuel shortages. Trains began to use timber and straw as fuel, instead of coal. In the winter of 1942, the 320km train journey from Killarney to Dublin took 23 hours! Tram services were cut back due to coal shortages. Private cars almost disappeared off the roads as petrol was in very short supply. Doctors were allowed petrol for emergencies. People walked, cycled or travelled in horse-drawn carriages again.

Fuel

People turned to other sources of energy such as peat and turf. The Phoenix Park was used to store supplies. Turf was gathered here and mounds of turf sometimes reached heights of almost 10m! Coal was very scarce. Gas and electricity were rationed during the Emergency and switched on only for a few hours each day.

Word Watch!
Glimmer Man
A Glimmer man went around to people's houses to check that they did not use gas at certain times. If people were caught using gas at the wrong time, they were fined immediately. Their gas supply was also switched off.

Ireland's Defence Forces

Irish Army

When World War II broke out, Ireland was almost defenceless. During the Emergency, there was a fear that the Germans or British would invade Ireland. In 1939, the Irish Army numbered just 7,600 and was very lightly armed. Soldiers wore a German style helmet until 1940 when it was replaced. The pay was low. A recruitment campaign increased the army's numbers during the war years.

Irish Navy

The Irish Navy had only two ex-fisheries vessels. They were responsible for coastal patrols and surveillance of German movement at sea.

Air Corps

In September 1939, the Air Corps had only 60 planes. Only a few hundred men served with the Air Corps. They observed and monitored air activity off Ireland's coastline.

Friendly Neutrality

During the war, around 170 aircraft crashed or landed in Ireland. British airmen who landed in Ireland were later allowed to travel over the border into Northern Ireland. However, Germans were imprisoned. Over 50,000 Irishmen served in the British army during the war.

Ireland is Bombed

In August 1940, a German aircraft dropped bombs on a creamery in Co. Wexford, killing three women workers and injuring many others.

Belfast was bombed by the Germans on 7 April 1941, killing over 700 people. It was bombed again on 4 May when 150 people were killed. Thirteen units of the Dublin Fire Brigade were sent up to Belfast to help put out the fires.

On the night of 31 May 1941, the Germans bombed the North Strand area of Dublin. The first bombs were dropped at 1.30am. Thirty-eight people were killed, ninety injured and over seventy homes destroyed. The German government apologised for the bombing and paid compensation to Ireland after the war. It said the air raid had been a mistake.

War is Over

When World War II ended in May 1945, Irish people were glad that they had stayed neutral throughout the war. People were horrified when they learned of the atrocities that occurred during the war. In May 1945, the British Prime Minister, Winston Churchill, delivered a speech criticising Ireland's neutrality. Three days later, the Irish population listened at their radios as De Valera responded in a radio broadcast.

> Mr Churchill makes it clear that, in certain circumstances, he would have violated our neutrality and that he would justify his action by Britain's necessity... All credit to him that he successfully resisted the temptation... Suppose Germany had won the war, had invaded and occupied England... she was finally brought to... let England go, but not the whole of England, all but, let us say, the six southern counties... Let us suppose further, that after all this had happened, Germany was engaged in a great war... would Mr Churchill... lead this partitioned England to join with Germany in a crusade? I do not think Mr Churchill would... Could he not find in his heart the generosity to acknowledge that there is a small nation that stood alone not for one year or two, but for several hundred years against aggression... a small nation that could never be got to accept defeat and has never surrendered her soul?

1. Under what circumstances do you think Churchill would have 'violated our neutrality'?
2. What comparison does De Valera make to help Churchill understand Ireland's neutrality?
3. Why, do you think, did De Valera give this speech?

Question Time

1. When did World War II break out?
2. What countries made up the Allied side?
3. Why, do you think, did Ireland remain neutral?
4. What were the advantages of being neutral?
5. What were the disadvantages of being neutral?
6. What other countries remained neutral during World War II?
7. Who was the Taoiseach of Ireland during the Emergency?
8. Why, do you think, was censorship introduced?
9. What food was rationed during the Emergency?
10. What methods of transport did people use during the Emergency?
11. What did Irish people use as fuel during the Emergency?

Creative Time

1. Imagine that you are working as a reporter in Dublin in 1941. Write the front page of the newspaper reporting on the bombing of the North Strand. Include a catchy title to attract the readers' attention. Include interviews with witnesses to the bombing and give opinions as to why you think Dublin was bombed.
2. Many English children were evacuated to Ireland to keep them safe during the war. Imagine that you were to be evacuated. What might you have brought with you in your suitcase?

Puzzle Time

Work out how much tea, butter, sugar and milk your family eat in a week. Compare that to the weekly allowance allowed in your ration book during the Emergency. How would your family have survived on these rations?

Food	Ration
Tea	14g
Butter	170g
Sugar	225g
Milk	1 litre

Time Detective

Working as an historian, study the front page of *The Irish Times*, 8 May 1945.

1 What shape are the photographs arranged in?

2 What, do you think, does this letter stand for?

3 How did this get through the censorship board?

4 Can you name the people in the photographs?

 **Web Watch!**

http://www.rte.ie/laweb/brc/brc_1940s_a.html
http://www.bbc.co.uk/history/ww2children/

Integration Project

The Emergency

English
Read some novels set in World War II such as *V is for Victory* by Sylvia Whitman, *Number the Stars* by Lois Lowry and *The Diary of Anne Frank*.

Gaeilge
Tá tú i do chónaí in Éirinn sa bhliain 1940. Scríobh do scéal i ndialann. Cad iad do chuid smaointe? Cad a cheapann tú faoin gcogadh?

Mathematics
During World War II, important messages were sent by radio in code. Read the Codemaker's Guidelines at
http://www.pbs.org/wgbh/nova/teachers/activities/pdf/2101_codebrea.pdf
Encode your own message. See if your friends can break your code and decipher your message.

Drama
Working in pairs, present a live radio broadcast that could have taken place during the Emergency. What important event are you covering? How will you handle censorship?

Geography
Using a blank map, mark in the Allies and the Axis powers in different colours.

SPHE
What is tolerance? Create a graffiti wall on 'Peace is …'. Using a large poster page, create a brick wall. Each member of the class fills in his/her own brick with his/her thoughts.

Art
Design a wartime poster encouraging people to ration their food and clothes during the war. Think of a good slogan for your poster. What images will you include?

Science
Investigate the invention of radar and sonar systems. Both of these systems send out waves and help with distance, speed and size of a target.

12 Children of War

Facts
- Every three minutes, one child dies in armed conflict.
- Over the last ten years, 1.6 million children have been killed in armed conflict throughout the world.
- Four million children have been disabled.
- More than one million children have been left orphaned or separated from their parents.
- It is estimated that about 300,000 children under the age of eighteen are still participating in armed conflicts around the world.

Children are innocent victims of war. They lose parents or are injured or killed in the crossfire. Some are forced to join armies and fight as soldiers. Many are captured and imprisoned. Others die of starvation.

Anne Frank and Zlata Filipovic lived through wars. They wrote about their experiences. Read their diaries to learn about the horrors of war they experienced.

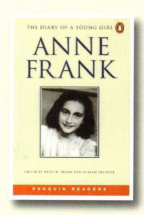 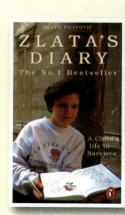

Children explore the lives of innocent victims of war and investigate the lives of Anne Frank and Zlata Filipovic

The Diary of Anne Frank

Anne Frank was a Jewish girl living in Amsterdam, Holland, during World War II. On her 13th birthday, she received a present of a red-and-white tartan diary. She named her diary 'Kitty'. On 6 July 1942, Anne and her family had to go into hiding from the Germans for fear of being sent to a concentration camp. During her two years in hiding, Anne wrote in her diary every day. Eventually, she and her family were found by the Germans. Anne later died in a concentration camp.

Word Watch!
Concentration Camps
Concentration camps were prisons that were set up by the Germans in order to get rid of certain people. More than six million Jews were killed in the concentration camps during the war. They were put into gas chambers to be poisoned.

24 December 1943
'Believe me, if you've been shut up for a year and a half, it can get to be too much for you sometimes. But feelings can't be ignored, no matter how unjust or ungrateful they seem. I long to ride a bike, dance, whistle, look at the world, feel young and know that I'm free, and yet I can't let it show.'

11 April 1944
'The time will come when we'll be people again and not just Jews! ... We can never be just Dutch, or just English, or whatever, we will always be Jews as well. And we'll have to keep on being Jews, but then, we'll want to be.'

15 July 1944
'I see the world being slowly transformed into a wilderness. I hear the approaching thunder that, one day, will destroy us too, I feel the suffering of millions. And yet, when I look up at the sky, I somehow feel that everything will change for the better, that this cruelty too will end, that peace and tranquillity will return once more.'

Zlata's Diary

Zlata Filipovic was an eleven-year-old girl living in Sarajevo. She called her diary 'Mimi'. She wrote in her diary from 1991 to 1993 about the war in Bosnia. Unlike Anne Frank, Zlata and her family survived the war and escaped. She came to live in Dublin.

Sunday, 12 April 1992
'I keep thinking about the march I joined today. It's bigger and stronger than war. That's why it will win. The people must be the ones to win, not the war, because war has nothing to do with humanity. War is something inhuman.'

Monday, 29 June 1992
'That's my life! The life of an innocent eleven-year-old schoolgirl! A schoolgirl without school, without the fun and excitement of school. A child without games, without friends, without the sun, without birds, without nature, without fruit, without chocolate or sweets, with just a little powdered milk. In short, a child without a childhood. A wartime child. I now realise that I am really living through a war, I am witnessing an ugly, disgusting war. I and thousands of other children in this town that is being destroyed, that is crying, weeping, seeking help, but getting none. God, will this ever stop, will I ever be a schoolgirl again, will I ever enjoy my childhood again? I once heard that childhood is the most wonderful time of your life. And it is. I loved it, and now an ugly war is taking it all away from me.'

Monday, 2 August 1993
'Some people compare me with Anne Frank. That frightens me, Mimmy. I don't want to suffer her fate.'

Question Time

1. Name some of the ways in which war can affect children.
2. Why did Anne Frank's family go into hiding?
3. What would you miss if you were forced to hide in a secret room?
4. What did Anne Frank call her diary?
5. What did Zlata Filipovic call her diary?
6. What are the similarities and differences experienced by Anne Frank and Zlata Filipovic?
7. Which entry, do you think, is the most moving and powerful? Why?

Creative Time

1. This is an extract from Anne Frank's diary:

> **8 July 1942**
>
> 'Margot and I started packing our most important belongings into a satchel. The first thing I stuck in was this diary, and then curlers, handkerchiefs, schoolbooks, a comb and some old letters. Preoccupied by the thought of going into hiding, I stuck the craziest things in the satchel, but I'm not sorry. Memories mean more to me than dresses.'

Imagine that you had to go into hiding for a long time like Anne Frank. You are only allowed to take three items with you. What three things would you take with you? Give reasons why you selected these things.

2. Imagine that you were given the opportunity to interview either Anne Frank or Zlata Filipovic. Write the questions that you would like to ask.

Puzzle Time

True or **False**?
Working in small groups, discuss the following statements. You must each justify your ideas and then come to a group agreement. Organise a class discussion comparing your decisions.

1. Children of the age of 16 should be allowed to join the army. _____
2. Children should be evacuated from war-torn countries. _____
3. War is inevitable. _____
4. War affects children more than adults. _____
5. War is inhuman. _____

Time Detective

Working as an historian, read one of the diaries in more detail and share the experiences the girls lived through.

Web Watch!

The Anne Frank house, Amsterdam
http://www.annefrank.org/

Official Anne Frank Website
http://www.annefrankguide.net/

Integration Project

Children of War

English
Imagine that you are one of the girls. Write a diary entry telling about your day. How do you feel? What are your thoughts, fears and hopes?

Gaeilge
Scríobh i ndialann phearsanta faoi do dheireadh seachtaine. Céard a tharla? Ar tharla aon rud suimiúil?

Mathematics
Anne Frank and her family went into hiding on 6 July 1942, until they were discovered on 4 August 1944. How long were the Franks hidden in their secret hiding place?

Drama
Hot Seat: One member of your class takes on the role of Anne Frank or Zlata Filipovic and sits in the 'Hot Seat'. Take it in turns to ask them questions. They must answer the questions in role.

Geography
On a map of Europe, trace the life of Anne Frank. She was born in Frankfurt, Germany, her family moved to Amsterdam, Holland, and then she was sent to a Concentration Camp in Bergen-Belsen, Germany.

Art
Design a new front cover for *The Diary of Anne Frank*. What important information will you include? What image will you draw?

SPHE
What other experiences of intolerance or prejudice can you think of? How can we help rid the world of this?

Science
How has new technology and inventions changed the face of war? What invention has had the most impact on war?

13 Ireland, the EU and the UN

1957
The European Economic Community (EEC) is established.

1990
The EEC becomes the European Community (EC). Germany united; East Germany joins as part of unified Germany.

2002
The Euro currency comes into use.

1950 — 1960 — 1970 — 1980 — 1990 — 2000 — 2010

1973
Ireland joins the EEC.

1992
The European Union (EU) replaces the EC.

2004
The EU expands with ten new member states.

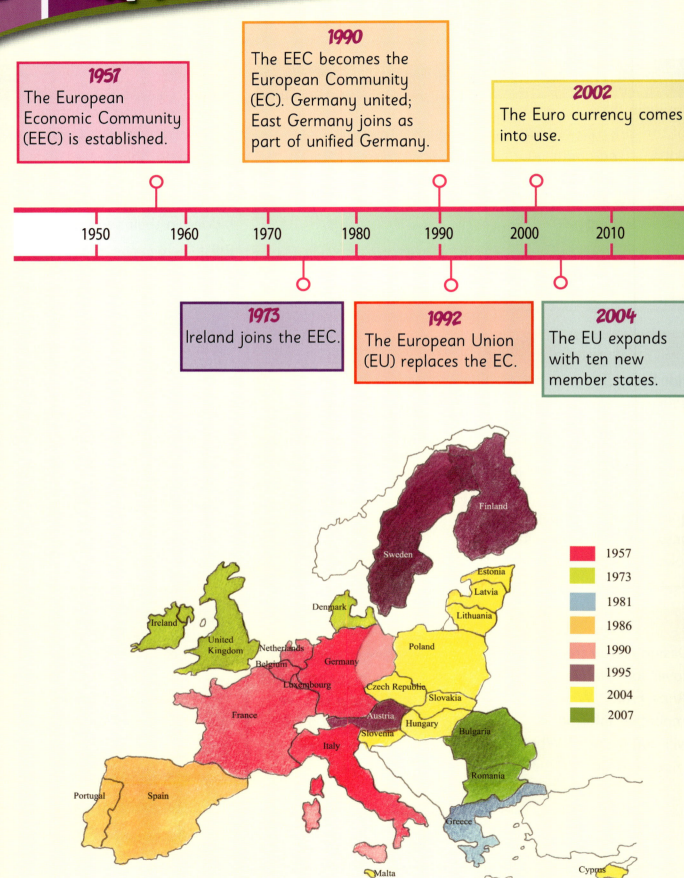

Legend:
- 1957
- 1973
- 1981
- 1986
- 1990
- 1995
- 2004
- 2007

Children develop a sense of personal, national, European and global identity as they explore the history of the European Union and the United Nations.

EU Factfile

Members: 27 – Ireland, Britain, France, Spain, Portugal, Italy, Austria, Hungary, Belgium, Luxembourg, The Netherlands, Germany, Denmark, Sweden, Finland, Greece, Czech Republic, Slovakia, Poland, Lithuania, Latvia, Estonia, Bulgaria, Romania, Cyprus, Malta and Slovenia

Official Languages: 23

Motto: *In Varietate Concordia* – United in Diversity

Currency: Euro. 15 of the 27 member states have adopted the Euro as their currency.

Anthem: Beethoven's 'Ode to Joy'

Europe Day: 9 May

Total Area: 4,422,773 sq km

Population: 490,426,060

Presidency: Each member state takes on the role of the Presidency for six months.

The EU flag has twelve gold stars in a circle. This symbolises unity, solidarity and harmony.

The euro is used by 15 member states.

The Founding Fathers

After the devastation of two world wars, the people of Europe wanted to work co-operatively to develop a lasting peace. On 9 May 1950, Robert Schuman proposed the establishment of a European Coal and Steel Community. This allowed a common market between France, Germany, Italy, Belgium, the Netherlands and Luxembourg. This idea was originally thought of by Jean Monnet. Schuman and Monnet are called the 'Founding Fathers of Europe'. In 1957, the Treaty of Rome established the European Economic Community (EEC). This allowed for a common market covering a wide array of goods and services.

Since Ireland joined the EU in 1973, it has received over 55 billion euro in grants. The EU has funded transport and communication developments, created employment, increased trading and helped the environment. Together, the countries of the European Union have a stronger voice in the world.

Robert Schuman and Claude Monnet

Word Watch!
Common Market

The Common Market is an agreement among countries to allow each country to trade freely with one another. Goods and services are 'common' to all – they can be brought from one country to another without payment of extra taxes.

The United Nations

The League of Nations which was set up after World War I, had failed. After World War II, some fifty countries met in San Francisco between April and June 1945. They drew up the Charter for the United Nations. On 24 October 1945, the United Nations (UN) was born. United Nations Day is celebrated on this day every year. The United Nations works to bring the countries of the world together for peace, justice, human dignity and the wellbeing of people. The UN has 192 members. Every member country has one vote, regardless of its size or power.

The UN emblem shows the world being held by the olive branches of peace.

San Francisco, June 1945

Signing the agreement, June 1945

> 'Oh, what a great day this can be in history! There were many who doubted that agreement could ever be reached by ... countries differing so much in race and religion, in language and culture... History will honor you [for writing the UN Charter]... If we had had this Charter a few years ago – and, above all, the will to use it – millions now dead would be alive. If we should falter in the future in our will to use it, millions now living will surely die... That we now have this Charter at all is a great wonder.'
>
> **Harry Truman**
> U.S. President, 25 June 1945.

United Nations flag 10 October, 1949

Today, the UN deals with a wide range of global issues, from combating disease to the education of young people. The member states of the UN working co-operatively are crucial to its success. The UN headquarters are in New York City.

United Nations Headquarters, New York

Question Time

1. Name the **six** members of the European Coal and Steel Community.
2. In what year did Ireland join the EEC?
3. What other countries joined at the same time as Ireland?
4. List all the member states of the EU.
5. Why, do you think, is Europe Day on 9 May?
6. When did the Euro come into use?
7. How has joining the EU affected Ireland?
8. Who were the founding fathers of the EU?
9. What is the emblem of the United Nations?
10. What is the aim of the United Nations?
11. Who is the Secretary-General of the United Nations today?
12. Where is the UN Headquarters?

Creative Time

1. Design a new flag for the European Union. What important images or symbols do you think should be included?

2. The UN relies on its members working co-operatively. They have a set of rules called a Charter. The member states must obey these rules. Make a Class Charter that will help your class work co-operatively and effectively. Working in small groups, write a set of rules that will help your class to work together and deal effectively with conflicts. Come together and listen to each group's rules. Agree on a class charter, including the most important rules.

3. Hold a model United Nations Conference. Each person takes on the role of a different country. Research your chosen country and be ready to represent it in your model UN Conference. As a class, choose three global issues that concern you the most. Debate these issues and come to an agreement on how best to effectively face these problems. Remember to work together to overcome the challenges.

Puzzle Time

On 10 December 1948, the United Nations adopted the Declaration of Human Rights. Fill in the missing words from this document.

slavery	colour	free	law
punishment	right	life	equal

Article 1: All human beings are born _____ and _____ in dignity and rights.

Article 2: Everyone is entitled to all the rights and freedoms… without distinctions of race, _____, sex, language, religion, political or other opinion…

Article 3: Everyone has the right to _____, liberty and personal security.

Article 4: No one shall be held in _____ or servitude.

Article 5: No one shall be subjected to torture or to cruel, inhuman or degrading treatment or _____.

Article 6: Everyone has the _____ to recognition everywhere as a person before the law.

Article 7: All are equal before the _____ and are entitled without any discrimination to protection of the law.

Time Detective

Working as a time detective, continue the EU timeline from page 96, writing the next five stops. What countries, do you think, will be the next new member states of the EU? What does the future hold for the EU? Predict the future developments in the EU along your timeline. Mark in the year that you think each development will happen.

Web Watch!

Take the EU and UN quiz at:
www.bbc.co.uk/schools/citizenx/internat/eu/quiz.shtml

Play the UN game Food Force at:
http://www.food-force.com/

Play the UN Flag Game at:
http://www.cyberschoolbus.un.org/flagtag/frm_ft_intro.asp?score=0&screen_height=768

Integration Project

English
Play Word Tennis. Two players in turn must name a country in the EU. If they repeat a country already named or cannot name one, they must sit down.

Gaeilge
Tá tú ar do laethanta saoire san Eoraip. Scríobh carta phoist chuig do chara. Déan cur síos ar an aimsir. Cad atá á dhéanamh agat?

Mathematics
Examine the Euro currency. What images are on the different notes? Why, do you think, were they chosen? What images would you have chosen for the Euro notes?

English Creative Writing
Write an acrostic poem about the United Nations. Each line in the poem should begin with a letter of the words United Nations.

Ireland, the EU and the UN

Geography
How well do you know the EU and the UN? To test yourself, visit:
http://www.bbc.co.uk/schools/citizenx/internat/eu/quiz.shtml

Music
Hold a class Eurovision Song Contest. Divide your class into groups. Each group should take on the role of a European country. Write a song to perform in front of your class. Organise a class vote to find your Eurovision winner.

Art
Design a poster showing why your local area should be chosen as European Capital of Culture. How will you convince people to choose your town? How could you increase your local area's chances of winning? Include pictures and a catchy slogan.

Science
Write some important guidelines that the EU could adopt, encouraging respect and care for the environment. What changes would you suggest? Would you introduce penalties if guidelines were not followed?

14 Heroes from the Past

Who Am I?
With your class, list thirty historic figures that you have learned about. Each name is written on a piece of paper. One name is stuck onto the back of each member of the class. You have fifteen minutes to walk around your classroom asking questions to find out who you are. Each question can only be answered with yes or no. If you can guess who you are, you win. The person who does this in the quickest time is the overall winner.

Dinner Party
You have been given a once in a lifetime opportunity. You are hosting a dinner party for historic figures from the past. Think of all the interesting people you have learned about. You can invite any four figures to the party whether they are dead or alive. Think carefully about your decision. Once you have made your selection, plan the dinner party.

Children work as historians, investigating historic figures from the past.

Invitation
Design an invitation for your guests. What important information will you include on your invitation?

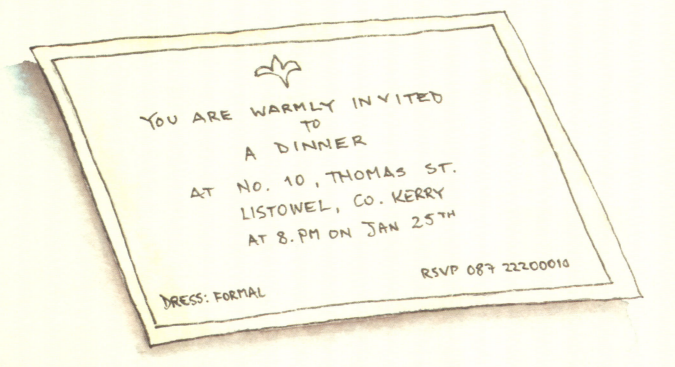

Menu
What food will you prepare for your guests? Remember some of your guests may be from a different era. Think carefully about each course. Will you prepare food that was popular in their time?

Seating Arrangement
Where will you seat your guests? Who would be best seated together? Which guests do you think would get on the best?

Conversation Topics
Prepare some topics that you think would create an interesting conversation. Think of the different interests of your varied guests.

Questions
Prepare one question to ask each guest. This is a rare opportunity to have your question answered so put a lot of thought into each question.

Heroes Gallery

Choose one historic figure who you think has achieved great things. Each member of the class chooses his/her own hero. These heroes could be sketched or photographs obtained. Under your hero, write the reason why you selected that person. All of the images could be hung along a clothes line to create a heroes gallery.

Who Am I?

Research an historic character you would like to find out more about. Write a diary for your character. You could take on the role of your historic character. Members of your class could ask you questions about your life.

Web Watch!

http://www.bbc.co.uk/history/historic_figures/

Integration Project

Heroes from the Past

English Oral Work
Create a news broadcast about your favourite hero from the past. What was his/her achievement? Working in groups, assign different roles such as presenter, director, researcher and hero.

Gaeilge
Fiche Ceist: Smaoiníonn dalta ar dhuine éigin. Cuireann na daltaí ceisteanna air/uirthi chun fáil amach cén duine atá i gceist.

Mathematics
Discover which famous mathematician shares the same interests as you. To take the Maths Quiz, visit: http://nces.ed.gov/nceskids/grabbag/MathQuiz/

English Creative Writing
Write an A to Z booklet about famous heroes from the past. Try to include at least one historic figure for each letter of the alphabet.

Geography
Investigate local people who have made important contributions to your area. What service or industry do they work in? What special skill do they have?

Music
Investigate 'This Day in Music History'. What famous composers were born on this day? What was the Number One hit in the music charts on this day? To find out, visit: http://www.datadragon.com/day/

SPHE
What historic figure do you admire the most? Why do you admire him/her? How has that person influenced you?

Science
Investigate famous scientists from the past. Explore the life of one scientist who interests you. For information, visit: http://www.famous-scientists.net/

15 Quiz Time

Now it is quiz time. Your class can answer the quiz in small groups of four or write the answers by yourself.

Round One: Story
1. Where did Anne Frank live?
2. What did Anne Frank call her diary?
3. Why did Anne Frank's family have to go into hiding?
4. Where did Zlata Filipovic live?
5. What did Zlata call her diary?
6. What tribe did Nekumonta belong to?
7. What tragedy came to Nekumonta's village?
8. What difficult mission did Nekumonta set out on?
9. Who was Manitou?
10. Why did the animals help Nekumonta in his search?

Round Two: Early Civilisations
1. Who were the first people to live in America?
2. How did they reach the continent of America?
3. What is a teepee?
4. What food did the Native Americans eat?
5. Why were the Native Americans called Indians by the Europeans?
6. Who were the first people to settle in New Zealand?
7. Who was the first explorer to discover New Zealand?
8. What does *Aotearoa* mean?
9. Which bird was hunted to extinction by the Maoris?
10. What is the Maori war dance called?

Children revise and consolidate information that they have learned.

Round Three: A Time of War
1 In what year did World War I begin?
2 Why, do you think, was the war called 'The Great War'?
3 What countries were known as the Allied Forces?
4 What countries were known as the Central Powers?
5 What was the land between the trenches known as?
6 When did World War II break out?
7 Who was the Taoiseach in Ireland during World War II?
8 Why, do you think, did Ireland remain neutral?
9 Why was the European Union formed?
10 What is the aim of the United Nations?

Round Four: The Renaissance and O'Connell
1 What does 'Renaissance' mean?
2 When did the Renaissance occur?
3 Who were the Renaissance Men?
4 List **two** of their works.
5 Why was the invention of the printing press so important?
6 Who was called the Liberator?
7 What is Catholic Emancipation?
8 What was 'Catholic rent'?
9 When was Catholic Emancipation finally granted?
10 Why did O'Connell cancel the Monster Meeting planned for Clontarf?

Round Five: Farming and Transport
1 Where was the first farming community in Ireland located?
2 What crops did they grow?
3 When did the first farmers arrive in Ireland?
4 Why did the arrival of the potato have such a huge influence on the Irish diet?
5 Name **three** types of early bicycles.
6 Who invented *The Rocket*?
7 Where was the first railway line in Ireland?
8 When did the Luas begin operating in Dublin?
9 Who is often called the 'Father of Flight'?
10 Who carried out the first successful flight in Kitty Hawk in 1903?

Round Six: Name these historic figures

Score: /56

Web References

Chapter	Topic	Website reference
1	My Locality through the Ages	http://www.rootsweb.ancestry.com/~nirfer/ http://www.irelandgenweb.com/special.htm
2	Farming through the Ages	http://www.historyforkids.org/learn/economy/farming/ http://www.dmoz.org/Kids_and_Teens/School_Time/Science/Farming/ http://www.teagasc.ie http://www.esatclear.ie/~turoefarm/top/farms.htm
3	Native Americans	http://nativeamericans.mrdonn.org/stories/index.html. http://www.mce.k12tn.net/indians/games/native_american_games.htm http://www.americanwest.com/pages/indrank.htm
4	The Healing Waters	http://www.native-languages.org/kids.htm http://www.42explore2.com/native4.htm http://www.mainlesson.com/display.php?author=olcott&book=indian&story=hidden
5	The Maoris	http://maaori.com/people/maoriara.htm http://www.maori.org.nz/ http://www.newzealand.com/travel/about-nz/culture/haka-feature/haka.cfm http://www.aucklandnz.com/
6	The Renaissance	http://www.renaissanceconnection.org/main.cfm http://www.activehistory.co.uk/Miscellaneous/free_stuff/renaissance/frameset.htm
7	Remembering School	http://www.primaryscience.ie/site/activities_school_websites.php http://www.kildare.ie/library/ehistory/2007/10/naas_convent_of_mercy_primary.asp
8	The Liberator	http://multitext.ucc.ie/d/Daniel_OConnell http://www.clarelibrary.ie/eolas/coclare/people/daniel.htm
9	Planes, Trains and Automobiles	http://www.cybersteering.com/trimain/history/ecars.html http://www.cie.ie/about_us/schools_and_enthusiasts.asp#1 http://www.century-of-flight.net/ http://www.discoverychannel.co.uk/cars/timeline/
10	World War I	http://www.bbc.co.uk/schools/worldwarone/observer/ http://www.bbc.co.uk/schools/worldwarone/hq/trenchwarfare.shtml http://www.warmuseum.ca/cwm/games/overtop/index_e.html
11	The Emergency	http://www.rte.ie/laweb/brc/brc_1940s_a.html http://www.atireland.ie/inclusive/assets/pdf/ireland_in_ww2_6hats.pdf http://www.bbc.co.uk/ww2peopleswar/stories/71/a4497771.shtml
12	Children of War	http://www.annefrankguide.net http://www.icrc.org/eng/children http://www.warchildren.org/
13	Ireland, the EU and the UN	http://europa.eu/index_en.htm http://ec.europa.eu/economy_finance/netstartsearch/euro/kids/index_en.htm http://www.bbc.co.uk/schools/citizenx/internat/eu/quiz.shtml http://www.food-force.com/
14	Heroes from the Past	http://www.famous-scientists.net/ http://www.bbc.co.uk/sn/tvradio/programmes/horizon/broadband/broadband_only/heroes/ http://www.bbc.co.uk/history/historic_figures/

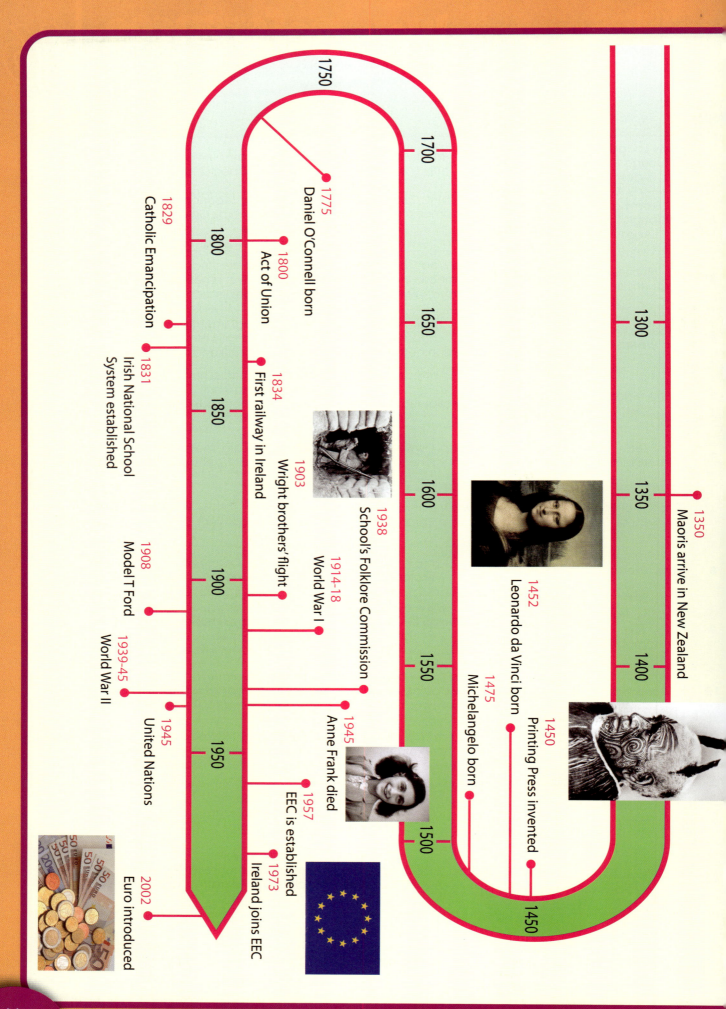